Among My KLEDIMENTS
June Carter Cash

© by Jim Marshall

Among My KLEDIMENTS
June Carter Cash

ZONDERVAN PUBLISHING HOUSE
OF THE ZONDERVAN CORPORATION
GRAND RAPIDS, MICHIGAN 49506

Photographs used in this book may not be used in any way without permission of the copyright holder.

Diligent effort has been made to determine the source of all photographs and to obtain the necessary permission. If such acknowledgment has been inadvertently omitted, the author and publisher would appreciate receiving full information so that proper credit may be given in future editions.

All songs and poems in this book are copyrighted © by House of Cash, Inc., Hendersonville, Tennessee, and may not be used without permission of the copyright owner.

AMONG MY KLEDIMENTS
© 1979 by June Carter Cash
This edition 1981
Library of Congress Cataloging in Publication Data
Cash, June Carter, 1929-
    Among my klediments.

    1. Cash, June Carter, 1929-   2. Country musicians—United States—Biography.   3. Christian biography—United States.   I. Title.
ML420.C2653A3   784'.092'4 [B]   79-10959
ISBN 0-310-38171-1

All rights reserved. No part of this publication may be reproduced, stored in a retrieval system, or transmitted in any form or by any means, electronic, mechanical, photocopy, recording, or otherwise, without the prior permission of the publisher.

Printed in the United States of America

To
JOHNNY CASH
husband, lover, friend,
and brother-in-Christ

Contents

The Early Years • 13

Ambition • 57

Johnny Cash • 79

Home & Children • 109

Special Moments & People • 133

Introduction

"I've got to go home among my klediments," I've heard them say—those precious mountain people in southwestern Virginia and eastern Tennessee.

A klediment can be almost anything that has earned a right to be a part of things close to you. It can be precious antique furniture gathered from grandmother, pieces of china, little handmade doilies, the straw mats on your floor, or the priscilla curtains you made yourself. A klediment can be a thing you love.

A klediment can be an old ace bandage that saw you through two months of a sprained ankle, a faded parking ticket, a jar of screws. A klediment can be a thing you just won't throw away.

A klediment can even be the water bugs behind the kitchen sink, the wood in the woodbox, or the witch hazel in the medicine chest.

A klediment can be a person dear to you.

In these pages I want to share with you some things which are very precious to me, my loved ones and loved things, my hard times and good times—just an album of my klediments and my spiritual highs and lows.

The Early Years

I would lie upon my back searching the clouds for the face of Jesus. The mountains formed a frame for the sky that was mine, and many times I thought I saw His face. It changed from one profile to another, but always it was the face of Jesus and very special to me. For no one else could see it. I felt the world was mine and I was His only speck of sand. I was Christ's only creation and very special to Him.

I would do wonderful things someday. I would leave these mountains, and by some miracle with some marvelous kind of wisdom I would make kings and queens, presidents and other important people ask my advice and listen to me. I would share with them this wonderful world of Christ that was mine. They would understand, and peace would rule the world.

Such a dream. . . .

Our big white nine-room house hugged the side of Clinch Mountain in southwestern Virginia at a little place called Maces Spring. We heard the crickets, the frogs, and the old steam whistle of the train coming down that lonesome valley. The house had a porch on three sides, with tall boxwood hedges framing the yards, and all kinds of blue spruce and pine, and a pond just to the left where the creek was dammed up coming out of the mountain.

My mother, Maybelle Carter, had come from the other side of the mountain, the Copper Creek side, and she was considered a "hard worker." She gave birth to two of us girls, Helen and I, without the help of even an aspirin and only my Grandma Carter as a midwife. But then Grandma Carter had had nine children, so I guess she was a help. Only when Anita was born did they send for Doctor Meade, who came in his horse and buggy from Mendota. Everyone was sad and scared, and they sent Helen and me over the hill to a neighbor—and *they* were all crying.

Later I learned that Mama had almost died. Anita weighed ten and a half pounds, and mother was just over five feet tall. I believe they did give her an aspirin that time.

Mother was good stock, a thoroughbred from the Addington family, and she wouldn't have been much of a mountain woman if she'd gone off to the hospital to have her babies.

The Addingtons from Copper Creek had come to Culpepper County from England in 1773. Later they moved to Scott County and settled to be farmers, storekeepers, and schoolteachers. Mother's people had been quite wealthy in England, some in Parliament, and one ancestor was even buried at Richmond Palace. He was Henry Addington, prime minister the term before William Pitt. Wellington attributed his defeat of Napoleon to advice given him by Henry Addington. It was probably the best thing Henry ever did because he was a very unpopular prime minister for a short time.

The Addingtons had big English-style, two-story houses in Copper Creek, with cellars where they buried cabbages, potatoes, and put sauerkraut in huge jars. They had ice houses; they cut the ice from the river in the winter and stored it in sawdust for summer. They lived in a world of sheep, guinea hens, turkeys, ducks, and brine pickles—and geese of all things.

The folks in Clinch Valley never did all those things.

They called Clinch Valley "Pore Valley"—it was the other side of the mountain, the Carter side. If you ran a high fever in Clinch Valley, the men took to the mountains to kill a squirrel. The women would boil the squirrel with dumplings, and the broth from the squirrel and dumplings would cure anything from smallpox to whooping cough.

We seemed to have a lot of apples on our side of the mountain—probably because my daddy planted them all there. The women canned food from the garden for the winter months. And hogs—everybody had hogs.

Hogs were everywhere. And in the fall they were hung by their hind quarters and then lowered into a barrel of scalding water which helped to remove the hairs before butchering. Finally the hogs wound up in our smokehouse.

I don't know why we called them smokehouses. We never used smoke in them. We cured hams with salt, brown sugar, molasses, and black pepper. And when the meat was cured, we had side meat for the green beans or pinto beans or October beans, whichever beans we had that day.

I used to wonder why the people in our valley never killed a beef or sheep or lamb. Meat meant hog to me until I crossed to the other side of the mountain.

This was the world I was born into—the two different valleys. The people in both valleys were poor, had plenty to eat, and they all feared God.

About 1914, A. P. Carter had gone to the Copper Creek side of the mountain from the Clinch side, had seen Sara Dougherty singing and playing her autoharp on Mill Nichol's front porch, had fallen in love and brought her back to the Clinch Mountain side as his wife.

Maybelle, Sara's first cousin, came to visit Sara. Ezra Carter, A. P.'s brother, saw her, loved her, and married her in her sixteenth year in Bristol, Virginia. Maybelle began to sing with Sara and A. P., and thus came the original singing Carter Family to the mountains of Virginia.

They were to make their first record in Bristol in August, 1927, and they were to become the first family ever elected to the Country Music Hall of Fame. They gathered, wrote, and recorded some 350 songs that have formed a basis for country music as we know it today. Many an old Elizabethan ballad would have been lost but for the perseverance of my Uncle A. P. and his desire to preserve those songs. His world was music, sawmills, farms, and fruit trees, and he was the official head of the singing Carter Family.

When I was a little girl I cried a lot about the "Father of Dewey Lee," "The Cyclone of Rye Cave," and "My Clinch Mountain Home"—mostly songs about real people who lived nearby and had died in some tragic manner or of a broken heart. That simple little Carter Scratch, a guitar style perfected by my mother, gave the songs an eerie sound, and I really thought everybody had a mother who played a guitar, and an Aunt Sara who came with her autoharp to play and sing, and an Uncle A. P.

Uncle A. P. always had a bunch of songs in his pocket wrapped in yellow paper—and he always wanted my chair. There was no way I could find a chair of my own; they all seemed to be just where he wanted to sit. I spent a good part of my childhood moving out of Uncle A. P. Carter's chair.

I was born June 23, 1929, and my birth certificate read "Valerie June Carter—Health: Good." I was in the middle—Helen was the oldest and Anita the youngest.

When I was about five years old, I would ride behind my daddy on his motorcycle. I rode all the way to Kingsport, Tennessee, behind Daddy, holding on for dear life and squealing with delight, my hair streaming in the breeze. There was no fear in me anywhere, even when Daddy ran his motorcycle into the ditch and I sailed into a corn field. I survived with only scratches and an eager yearning to do anything my father did—to follow him and do anything his boy would have done. Only I wasn't a boy. I was a girl. But I really tried hard not to be. I wanted to be Daddy's boy.

My daddy, Ezra Carter, was an important man. He would take the train or ride his motorcycle to Bristol, Virginia, where he was a railway mail clerk. From Bristol he'd ride the train to Washington, D. C., with the registered mail. And he carried a gun. He got a check every month from the government which he immediately spent at fifty cents or a dollar a day to anyone from the valley who would work for him.

Daddy had a basement dug under our big old house. He had a road built to the top of the mountain. He dammed up the Holston River to make more power for the homemade generator he had improvised. He set out apple orchards. He did everything and anything that would share his check with the people in our valley. Because we were all poor. The neighbors were poor because it was the Depression and they had no work and only their tobacco money once a year, if they had an allotment.

You were lucky if you had a half-acre allotment from the government to raise tobacco. If you grew four extra rows, a nice government man with a silly grin on his face would come and hack it down. They wanted no surplus of tobacco so they could keep the prices up.

Yes, they were poor, and we were poor because of Daddy's projects. But that government check went a long way, and we all ate well during the crawling-out from under the Depression.

Some winters when the country hams were gone from the smokehouse and the cupboard seemed a little bare, we'd take the shotgun and head for the mountain in search of a rabbit. But sometimes even the rabbits were scarce.

THE HUNT

O Lord, it's hungry here this year,
Not a hippity to be found.
I searched in all the brush piles
And poked holes in the ground.
I even took my slingshot
And went down by the trees,
They always found it safe there
Right close to the bees.
I always used to find one there,
Soon his hide would be hung,
I'd kill him quiet and easy
And only twice get stung.
But things they've gone from
   bad to worse,
There's nothing left to cook.
I looked most everywhere to no avail,
So I finally searched a book.
I read about a catfish that walks
   up over land;
A catfish stew would taste real good,
And we need a few on hand.
So send him on this way, Lord,
Walking with flippers on the go,
And I'll take my little slingshot
And I'll track him in the snow.

MY DADDY

He built a road up old Clinch Mountain, all the way to the top.
It didn't really go nowhere, just up there to a rock,
But he planted apples, peaches, grapes, and pears,
We didn't go up too often for there were snakes and bears.
And we didn't have any electric lights—we warmed by an old fireplace,
No running water, no bathroom—we took it in the face.
But things they got better; Daddy dammed up the branch,
The water wheel would roll and electricity took a chance,
For half the wires were burned in two and the lights kept going out,
For late at night sometimes it stormed and the poles they knocked about.
He put a cement tub down in the washhouse, and there we took our bath.
We had a potbellied stove to warm us—we were one of them that hath.

Mount Vernon Church should have been a Methodist church according to the book, but it was the only church in our valley so we all enjoyed being Baptist, Presbyterian, Episcopalian, and Pentecostal. All the ministers preached there, sometimes all on the same Sunday. The valley people sang, shouted, and praised God in a God-fearing manner.

I grew up being afraid to wear make-up, afraid to dance, afraid to wear a basketball suit because it wasn't modest. I learned that I shouldn't use peroxide on my hair or go to beer joints. That's why I was so surprised about Daddy, I guess. It just never dawned on me that my daddy would take a drink of liquor.

It was on one of my trips down to the gully to the place we called "the toilet" that I found it.

Now the toilet was a building you would never put near the house because it always smelled of lime and other things. To reach it you had to walk over the little dam, past the workshop, the blacksmith shop, and down the gully. While we were there we caught up on fashion and what the world had to offer in the Sears and Roebuck catalog. I remember seeing that you could buy the Carter Family records there in that catalog.

Well, it was on one of my trips there that I found it—right behind the toilet—as big as life—a dirty old bottle of liquor hidden in the bushes.

I ran across the dam dragging that bottle with me, hollering, "Daddy, Daddy, somebody left a terrible bottle of whiskey behind our toilet. Daddy, I have it here with me—"

He ran to meet me, and I'm sure he was trying to figure a way to save his precious bottle and its contents. But just as he reached me, I sailed that thing out over the water wheel and it broke into a thousand pieces. He never said a word to me, just hung his head and walked slowly toward the shop, with me trailing along, hollering, "Who do you think that terrible person could have been, Daddy? Who could have been so bad to bring that horrible old liquor and hide it behind the toilet? You'd whip him, wouldn't you, Daddy? I know you would. You'd give it to him hard."

I think I got to Daddy a little that day, but it was really Grandma Carter who put the end to his drinking.

My grandmother, Mollie Carter, always had something for me to do. I'd hear her before I reached the spring in front of her house. "Here comes a little girl just the right size to get me a bucket of water." I was just the right size for almost everything—like milking the cows or getting the kindling wood.

And Grandma Carter was just the right size, too.

Daddy would sometimes go into the mountains and stay all afternoon. I remember him coming out late one day with Uncle Grant—both in their panama hats—and Daddy's red eyes gave him away. It was then I realized that the terrible bottle I'd heaved away with great gusto had been his.

Soon after that, Grandma Carter fixed Daddy good. She went into the mountains one day and came out pulling a big copper kettle hooked over the end of a stick, dragging it downhill all the way, calling, "Ezra, Ezra, come here, Ezra. I've found the dandiest copper kettle for making apple butter." She neglected to mention all the copper tubing that went with the rest of that still. But Daddy's still days were over, and we had dandy apple butter that winter.

Grandma Carter was just the right size to put her son Ezra in his place. After that, we began to see Daddy standing outside the Mount Vernon Church on Sundays, and we knew he was hearing the Word of God and that everything would be all right.

Mount Vernon Church would ring on Sundays with songs of joy and praise. You could hear Grandpa Carter hollering "Amen" from the amen corner and Grandma belting out "The Land of the Uncloudy Day" —uncloudy with a 'y,' loud and clear. You could hear Grandma above everybody else, all the way to Maces Spring.

On Sundays we sang the "Hallelujah Chorus" for Daddy and listened, as did all the valley through the public address system he had set up, to Mozart, Beethoven, and Brahms. We also listened to him read the Bible. There would be no more whiskey stills for sure. My daddy was a Christian now, and he began collecting a great library of Christian books that were to make him one of the wisest men I'd ever known.

The church fell silent during the week except when the bell tolled the death of some person in the valley. Then all would go to dig the grave and share in the grieving for the loved one gone to a better land "across the river." I can't remember a funeral where anyone died and went to hell—although on Sundays the preachers preached to save the souls of all the lost sinners, and we cried and prayed for their salvation. Somehow we had the satisfaction that all had ended well in death and they were secure "in the arms of Jesus."

Then, life to me was four square miles of going to grandmother's, over to aunts and uncles, worming tobacco, hoeing corn, and milking cows. It was a world of pawpaws, chinka-pins, and huckleberries. Somewhere out there, over the mountains, there was a world I'd only seen in books. It was full of hamburgers, ice cream cones, and movie stars. Out there the preacher let you play basketball, and you could buy a real tube of lipstick—and you could dance. Somewhere over that mountain I could dance and it would be all right.

Once down on the Holston River I tried to swim across. It was a Sunday, and I had sewed up a hole in my bathing suit. Mama, Daddy, my sisters, and I were there. The current was strong and I started to struggle, finally going down. My life flashed by, and I could see myself sewing away on that old bathing suit on Sunday—against the will of God. That was all I could remember, except that I would miss my mother and my sisters. I settled into unconsciousness, sure I was going straight to hell.

I awoke to see the face of my father, and I marveled that God had spared such a sinner as me.

THE SIN

Don't dance, don't do that lady,
Don't you know that it's a sin?
The devil he is tempting you
Trying your heart to win.
My heart is yearning for the dance
My feet they get the itch,
But if I try it in the valley
They'll say that I'm a witch.

So I'll take my piece of chiffon cloth
And climb the mountain high.
I'll gather honeysuckle, laurel,
   and dogwood
Where only eagles fly.
I'll make myself a castle,
With flowers for the throne,
And I'll wrap my chiffon on me
And dance there all alone.

My soul will let the dance in,
My feet will start to fly,
I'll twirl and kick and laugh and sing
And reach up to the sky.
For laughing helps my heart somehow
And dancing makes me free—
We'll keep it from the valley
Just God and sin and me.

When you're thirteen or fourteen years old and you see a young man who makes you turn your head and look at him twice, all of a sudden you're not that little tomboy any more. You're a woman, and you want that man to look at you.

It seemed the devil had all kinds of ways to make the young men look at the young women with their lipstick, powder, and paint. But with all the preaching I'd heard, I thought I was probably the homeliest girl in Pore Valley. I'd observed the sinful side, and sometimes—Lord, help me—I had wishes of my own.

> He's gone to see old Eula Mae—
> I heard it at the store.
> He saw her at the beauty contest
> And he's gone to look some more.
> There's peroxide on her ringlets
> And lipstick, rouge and such,
> And if you stop and look at me,
> Friend, I just ain't that much.
> All covered up with church,
> My face all shiny bright,
> Why you can see me coming
> From fifty yards at night.
>
> I'll go sit on the big rock
> To see if he comes back.
> I'll gather me some polk berries
> And put them in a sack.
> I'll take some nice big red ones
> And rub them on my lips.
> I'll take some cotton from Mama's
>   quilts
> And pad it on my hips.
>
> For it's Eula Mae he's lookin' at
> While here alone I sit.
> Bring on the paint and powder—
> I need all I can get.

As a child, I didn't realize the Carter Family were special people. To me they were always plain Mother, Aunt Sara, and Uncle Doc (A. P.). And it was wonderful if you could sing like them.

My two sisters, Helen and Anita, had perfect pitch, but no matter how hard my mother tried or Anita pinched or Helen glared, I'd sing anywhere on the scale that my voice decided to go at that particular time. And it was never where they were.

When you don't have much of a voice and harmony is all around you, you reach out and pick something you can use. In my case, it was just plain guts. Since I couldn't sing, I talked a lot and tried to cover up all the bad notes with laughter. There wasn't much demand in that lonesome valley for the likes of me. Because a Carter could sing. All Carters sang—alto, tenor, lead, bass—all of them except me—on key.

And then, when I was about nine years old, I learned we were leaving the valley. I was going to see what it was like over the hill.

Mother was taking us to a place called Texas. She would be singing there with Aunt Sara and Uncle Doc. But the thing that scared me near to death was that I was to sing, too. Me—with Helen and Anita. I would have to endure Anita's pinches and Helen's glares and I would even have to learn to play the autoharp. What would I do? Why couldn't they let my cousin Janette sing? She and her brother Joe were going. Janette was Uncle A. P.

and Aunt Sara's daughter, and she could really sing. I could hit a rabbit on the run with a rifle, I could hitch a log to the traces, I could dance. But you couldn't do any of those things on the radio. I was afraid.

We loaded up our new Packard with all our klediments and started the trip to Texas, a million miles away.

I soon found out that the Texas people just didn't know much about life. They didn't even know what a poke was. Even Leonard Neal who had the store at Maces Spring had all kinds of pokes. I needed a poke to put my candy in. I tried in vain to get a poke. They just laughed at me. No one could understand my Appalachian dialect, and I sure couldn't understand theirs. Finally I walked around the counter and picked up my poke and found out those silly people called it a paper bag.

I ate my first ice cream cone. It was like a cookie all stuffed with ice cream. And my first grapefruit. I knew I must surely have the lockjaw!

At Hawthorne Junior High School in San Antonio, Texas, I had my first stage experience. I took my autoharp and my strong mountain dialect and marched right out in front of the whole school in the assembly hall and started singing away about "Old Engine 143." My big wrap-around pick got hung up in the strings. I pulled hard and the thing flew halfway across the stage. I never missed a word of the song, just a few notes on my harp, as I ran to retrieve my pick. Engine 143 wrecked successfully and so did my stage debut.

Three days a week we made transcriptions for Don and Dode Baxter in San Antonio. Helen played guitar and I played autoharp. Mother would never play with us, only with Aunt Sara and Uncle Doc, so even if our performance was bad we stood on our own and served our apprenticeship in the shadow of the famous Carter Family from the Mexican border stations.

I found out that life had roller skates to offer—real little wheels on your feet that rolled you down the street—movies on Saturday for five cents, and a little hat for my head on Sundays. And rattlesnakes at the zoo, where every Sunday afternoon they cooked one and you ate it if you had the nerve. Rattlesnakes were for biting people, not for eating. Mercy.

After about a year and a half in Texas, we came back to the valley, and I led a few years of my life like an ordinary girl. I went to church, studied, worked on the farm, milked cows, and helped raise chickens and wheat.

And I came to the realization that life has to end for all of us . . . .

He was not even a member of my family, but he was the father of my friend, Alice, and her grief was mine. I thought my heart would break. They told us to rejoice that he was in heaven, but that was hard for us to do because we grieved and hung onto his memory. And yes, we put up a fight. We took his death hard. He left a young wife and four children.

> We won't give up easily,
> We can't let him go.
> Why should he bless a world
> We don't even know.
> He's gone on to a land
> That's really out of sight,
> You've heard of people dying
>   of a broken heart—
> Oh, Lord, I think I might.
>
> Oh, give me, Lord, the grace
> That I might understand
> Life you give so easily
> And then you take the man.
> My heart is just too heavy,
> I'm falling to me knees.
> Help me accept the will of God—
> Oh, Lord, do help me please.

Helen, Anita, and I were young and scared when we started singing with Mother. We'd jump into the car and race to some schoolhouse or courthouse—going all over, singing till we were hoarse.

My sister Anita had great fingernails. And when she was young she had five dresses like the ones worn by the Dionne quintuplets and a Shirley Temple bowl and pitcher. She wore her hair in Shirley Temple curls, smiled and showed her dimples, won baby contests, and scratched like a panther. Even at six years old Anita had great fingernails. I know, because I bore the marks of those nails.

If your home had always been a house with several rooms and a yard to run and play in, the confinement of a two-seated Packard car could become either a prison or a palace of sorts. We really did have the house and yard—nestled back there against Clinch Mountain in Virginia—but we weren't always there. So that beautiful little Shirley Temple-looking sister of mine made our house on wheels either a palace or prison.

Anita was the princess with her two ladies-in-waiting, Helen and myself, in the back seat of the car. Her throne was several pillows—her own and Helen's and mine. We found ourselves at her feet much of the time in submission to the reigning princess of the day. But it really wasn't Anita's fault. We adored her. And so she used her subjects either by pinching or by singing too loud in my ear, reminding me I was off-key.

Mother and Aunt Sylvia (she was Daddy's younger sister and was singing with us) would ride in the front seat, the three of us in the back, and away we'd go to play the Kentucky or West Virginia coal-mining towns. And this was where the fingernails came in: How much singing of "Engine 143" or "Old Joe Clark" can you take? A six-year-old girl whose castle had tumbled and whose bones were aching from overcrowding could turn from an adored princess into a panther—and the fingernails went to work. Helen and I wore scratch marks all over both arms. We couldn't escape, so we just sat there while the curly headed one pinched and clawed away the frustrations of a six-year-old that should have been run off in the yard.

We petted her, bowed to her every whim, and she was a brat. I'll never know how she overcame it all. I guess traveling all those miles together in the back seat had a binding influence on the three of us that we couldn't explain. One day Anita was a brat; the next she was a cultured young lady. I don't know when the transition came. I don't even think she realized it when it did.

Then the back seat became a place where we learned to sing our parts. Helen always on key, Anita on key, and a good steady glare to remind me that I was a little sharp or flat. The scratches disappeared, and the traveling in the early days became a world of cheap gas stations, hamburgers, tourist homes, and old hotels with stairs to climb. We worked the Kemptime Circuit, the last of the vaudeville days, and the yearning to keep on singing or traveling just a little farther never left. The high school buildings gradually changed from little 300-seat auditoriums to the larger gymnasiums and halls. But we still could hear the original Carter Family transcriptions on many of the major radio stations as we traveled.

The traveling John and I do now with our own family is somewhat of a contrast. Gone are the overcrowded back seats, too many instruments and people— sometimes seven or eight in one car. But we didn't feel cramped at the time. It was a way of life, and the audience always enjoyed the live show. They rarely got to see one in those days. So in a way, we considered our life style very special—a binding of love, being together, and accomplishing something.

I wanted a permanent. All the girls had permanents. I hated the long curls that hung down my back, and I longed to sit under one of those fascinating permanent machines in Bristol that looked like some sort of monster. I would surely come out from under that contraption with the looks of Shirley Temple and go straight to Hollywood. I persisted until my weary mother finally took me to Bristol to the beauty shop.

They put my hair up in that thing, and it did wonders for me! The long auburn curls would never be the same again. I came out a changed girl. I had a fever of 105 degrees, my head was burned in several places, and the long auburn curls looked like some kind of an explosion in a mattress factory. I had the first victory haircut in the valley!

But you don't need pretty, long hair to shovel chicken manure or shock wheat or go logging on the mountain. Daddy said I should have been a boy, and I guess I was, at heart, the first few years of my life.

Hilton High School had a basketball team, and I wanted so much to be on it. I deserved to be on it. My name was Carter, and all Carters were great basketball players. The young men were usually tall and had perfect timing for hitting that old backboard, and the girls were fast on their feet. Some Carter was always on the all-county, all-state team.

I tried out, and I made the team. A coach wouldn't have the nerve not to put me on the team. I played guard. I guarded everybody—players, coaches, referees, spectators. I gave it all I had. Our gym floor was old pine lumber with splinters sticking up all over, and I usually carried a pretty good load of them around in me from sliding into everything. The Carters continued to win trophies for the state, but they were all cousins of mine, Lois, Fern, and Juanita.

They gave me a beautiful maroon and white basketball suit—very short—with white tennis shoes and white socks. I began to feel in my heart that a fourteen-year-

I had a cap with a bill and a pair of coveralls like the mechanics used to wear. I guess I felt better feeding the hogs and milking the cows in that kind of an outfit. But I felt really good in my coveralls when I was in the logging business.

My father bought every dogwood tree within twenty-five square miles. He'd found he could make a shuttle for the cotton mills out of the dogwood; he did this in his little shop over the garage over the blacksmith shop which wasn't too far from "the toilet."

And so Daddy and I took to the mountain to cut the dogwood. Now there was no way we could cut it all, but we worked hard at it for about four months. And during that time I learned about the logging business. But best of all I learned to drive the logging truck on that mountain road with the hairpin curves.

OLD BULL DOG

I learned to drive a logging truck
Out on old Baldy Ridge.
We sold the mules, hung up their traces,
And said good-by to Tim and Midge.
First in low, then on to second,
And finally on to high,
Down the mountain logs and logs
We bid the lumber bye.
It was a ton-and-one-half Chevrolet
With mud flaps in the back,
We'd chain the logs, maybe three or four,
And drag 'em in the track.

There was some big trees on the mountain
High by Hangman's Rock,
I'd take that old truck, throw her in gear,
And race up to the top.
I'd cut the biggest logs that'd ever
   been to town,
I'd gather them behind me,
And I'd drag 'em down.
I had my load, had started on,
And threw it into gear,
But the logs they got to rolling
And a'gaining on my rear.
I didn't know just what to do,
I had to fast make up my mind,
For twenty tons of rolling logs
Were right on my behind.

I thought about the Lord's Prayer
And mentioned Jesus' name,
I could hear the church bells ringing
And wondered who they'd blame.
I tried old high, then into second,
And rammed her into low,
But none of them did any good
'Cause I couldn't make her slow.

I came down that mountain
Like a greased pig on a stump—
Me, my truck, and five big logs
A'riding on my rump.

Don't ever drive a logging truck
With only three forward gears,
'Cause they've got another gear
That's hid—that'll take away your fears.
Oh, if I'd only had it,
I wouldn't have been bouncing like a frog,
So don't give me a logging truck
Unless it's got old Bull Dog.

old girl had a right to wear a basketball suit and sometimes a little lipstick. But in my ears I could always hear the preaching from old Mount Vernon Church that told me right from wrong, and I still had twinges of guilt about things like movies, lipstick, basketball uniforms, and dancing.

The summer I was fourteen, Mother Maybelle was off making music somewhere, and I began to ride with Uncle Flan Bays and his children and friends in the back of his old truck, across the mountain and down the valley to Carter's Valley and up above the Holston River. We went anywhere they had to sing because Uncle Flan taught singing school. I don't mean the pretty round notes, but square ones—crooked ones, shaped ones, do-re-me-fa-so-la-ti and all those funny looking ones. Each note on the scale had its own shape. And I finally learned to belt out a good clear alto. We'd go packed in the back of that old pickup, singing on the way to somewhere—Nora Lee, Vernon, Louise Wolf, Helen, Juanita—cousins, friends, young people.

I began to see that I had reached the age of accountability, as we called it. I was a young woman now, and it was my responsibility to start to choose between right and wrong. I was to account for my mistakes, and I was to be blessed if I chose the right way. But I felt lost. I carried a burden on my heart like a rock. I couldn't understand it. Was it the bathing suit I'd sewed up on Sunday? Was it the basketball suit and the lipstick I wore? Was it the dancing my feet yearned for? What was it?

I had heard the plan of salvation so many times, and it began to dawn on me that I had to change my life. I must be born again. Surely this lost feeling wasn't all those petty things I'd picked out as sin. It was just that I had to finally make a total commitment to God. I had to believe in Jesus and what He'd done for me. And I had to repent.

But I couldn't understand what I had to repent for. I wore out all the mourners' benches in Scott County that summer, and still I couldn't lift the conviction from my heart. I believed in Jesus, but I cried and prayed and begged and still found no total peace of mind. I felt I was surely bound for hell.

It happened at Uncle Flan Bays' house one night that summer I was fourteen. They were having prayer meeting, and there I was down on my knees again. I guess I was there until around midnight. I don't know what I expected. Some people receive the Holy Spirit very quietly indeed, but when I finally came into total submission to God, my feelings went off like an atomic blast. I shot up like an arrow, crying, singing, and the fire was all around me. I'd close my eyes and the flames still burned. I'd open them and there they were.

I believe I've been one of the fortunate few who've seen the tongues of fire as on the day of Pentecost. The Holy Spirit did truly enter my body, change me, and make me a new person. I was born again. I remember my mother shouting through the house, "My heart is so happy!"

It was one of the greatest summers of my life. I raised fifty-four acres of wheat—plowed it, sowed, it, cut it, shocked it, and worked with that thrashing machine. And I drove that logging truck.

I learned that girls didn't smoke, drink, or neck if they wanted to grow up to be ladies, and that their reputation was gone if they went out all alone in a car with a young man. And you really watched yourself for fear you'd be-

It was wonderful to be a mountain girl. My burden was lifted. My heart was free. And sometimes to get closer to nature I'd go to the spring to wash my hair in the cold mountain water.

I've gone and said something a lady shouldn't say,
But a hummingbird was buzzin' by and it flew
 this a-way.
You see, I'd washed my hair in the water by the spring,
And how was I to know I'd run into that thing.
I was all bent over on a rock
With my head all hanging down,
That hummingbird came in to look
And together we were bound.
He beat his wings about a thousand times a minute,
His little feet a-flyin' and my hair all hung up in it.
I tried some words like "shoo" and "scat"
And "hummingbird, please go,"
But the words didn't seem strong enough
So I let some more go.
I'd stop that little bird
If I could get my hair and it apart,
If I could just grab on,
There'd be someplace where I could start.
The more I hollered and cried for help
The more he threw a fit,
So I finally gave up on that bird
And choked the life right out of it.

Have you ever had your life just floatin' by,
And Satan grabbed it with a cry
And hung on like a hummingbird
And you just caught without a word?
For there's not really much you can say,
It's hard to run and get away,
You're stuck fast in the red-hot sin
And Satan claims where you have been.
There's only one way you can win—
You cut the bonds and let the Savior in.

come like some of the girls who smoked only in the rest room and lost the respect of all the boys in school. I always tried to take care that my peers thought well of me, and I'm thankful for the words my mother and father never said to me. It was just the way they lived that let me know it was my obligation to be a lady.

Most of all, I learned that God is love. I wasn't afraid any more. And I knew God was proud when I got that basketball back across the line. He forgot my sewing on Sunday, and He lifted me up and held me in the dance.

Daddy had to take an early retirement from the railroad because of low blood pressure. He encouraged us three girls to sing together, and he bought Helen an accordion and Anita a big bass fiddle that she had to stand on a chair to play, and I continued plucking my autoharp and tenor guitar. We had an offer from Drug Trade Products to do an early morning radio show from WBT, one of the top 50,000 watt stations in the country. The money was more than we ever dreamed of, and we really needed it with Daddy's early retirement so we decided to work a year with the Carter Family.

We moved with Mother, Aunt Sara, and Uncle Doc (A.P.) to Charlotte, North Carolina, and we lived in the Roosevelt Hotel on South Tryon Street because we couldn't find an apartment or a house. And we sang on WBT radio in the early mornings for Drug Trade Products with Grady Cole, our announcer.

We were all worried about the war. That war had knocked the Carter Family right off the front cover of *Life* magazine. We were scheduled to be on the cover the week of December 7, 1941, but Pearl Harbor took our place. I was to have been on that cover, too. A man from

New York City, who couldn't understand the way we talked, had come to photograph us with his stacks of flashbulbs in bushel baskets.

I listened to the music of "Paper Doll," watched the soldiers swarm the streets, marveled at their paratrooper boots, saw our country united in a sincere effort to bring peace to the world, and rode the Piedmont and Northern—a little narrow-gauge railroad—to Paw Creek school, about fifteen miles out in the country, because I missed the country people I loved. Most of all I missed my cousin Fern.

Everybody needs to have a cousin Fern. No one in the world had more freckles than me except my cousin Fern. I guess we looked alike, and we could wrestle each other and neither of us would ever win. I missed our rides on the Holston River in the flat-bottom boat. I missed the sound of the dogs running on the knob chasing some fox that may or may not have been there. I missed the big tenderloin hunks in the milk gravy that we had at Fern's house in the Little Valley. Her mother and father, Aunt Ora and Uncle Ermine, Daddy's brother, could always find a ham to cut or black walnuts to crack. The old log home where they lived in the Little Valley was the home of the Carters where my father and his brothers and sisters were born.* I missed it. I deserved to miss it. I was a Carter.

There were a lot of things that were different in Charlotte, North Carolina. Living in two adjoining rooms with a tiny attached kitchen was nothing like our big white home on the mountain, which we still owned. We tried in vain to find a house or an apartment, but there was nothing to be had, and we considered ourselves lucky to have even the little kitchen where we could still

---

It is now a national landmark.

fix hot biscuits and gravy before our early morning show.

The Johnson Family, the Briar Hoppers, the Tennessee Ramblers—gospel singers, western bands, and country bands—they were all there in person, and it was there I met Arthur Smith, a true friend for life. He wrote "The Fourth Man in the Fire," "I Saw a Man," "Dueling Banjos," and "Guitar Boogie." (Arthur and his wife, Dorothy, are two of our most devoted friends, and, like John and I, have committed their lives to God.)

We made the early morning walk to the WBT radio station, and Anita never woke up at all. She hugged the bedpost while I put on her jeans. I steered her through the streets to the station and up the elevator into the studio. She played her bass, sang right on pitch, then collapsed in the guitar case while Mother, Aunt Sara, and Uncle A.P. sang about "Lonesome Valley," "Church in the Wildwood," "Wildwood Flower," "Dixie Darling," and "Will the Circle Be Unbroken." They seemed to know thousands of songs and all of them by heart.

If I had trouble staying on key, Helen just hit that note a little harder. I'd never have made it through the days of radio without Helen. If I was off-key, she'd jump right on my part until I felt like getting off hers. She had graduated from Hilton High School before we moved to North Carolina and chose to take a post-graduate course with me out at Paw Creek where she could learn typing and shorthand and where they had a gym floor with no splinters.

Soldiers were everywhere, and I began to notice that they could see I was no longer a little girl, but was growing into a young woman.

I got asked for a date. That young man just marched right into the Roosevelt Hotel, straight up to my daddy, and asked him. I'd never been so scared in my life. No one asked my father anything, except maybe whether he had gotten his *Bristol Herald* or not. Most young men were frightened to death of him.

Helen also got asked for a date. To tell the truth, it was a double date. My father must have had a lot of excuses he could have used to say "no," for he had been planning them for years. But they all faded away behind that young man's confidence, and away we went to a ball game—in a car of all things. But I knew Daddy must feel pretty secure about our safety since Helen and I were together. That's the way we dated for years. Always together—Helen and I.

There didn't seem to be a church handy on Sundays, and we drifted into just not going. Then I was reminded again of God's might.

I don't even remember their names, just two young people, a soldier and his wife, who had a room down the hall from us. They had a tiny baby maybe three months old.

We had had a hard snow and the streets were paralyzed and the little baby started running a high fever. Mother Maybelle had lost her sister and father with pneumonia, and she knew the signs. No doctor could come, and we couldn't get to one. Then I remembered Grandma Addington telling me that the only thing to do for pneumonia was to use onion poultices—fresh onions sautéed and wrapped in cloth. Put that over the lungs, and with God's help a pneumonia victim just might live.

All night long as the snow continued to fall and the wind blew, I sat with that little couple or ran to our kitchen to make new poultices. Ran back again and again. But mostly I prayed. I just couldn't watch that little baby die. The mother cried all the time, and I acted brave, patted her, carried poultices, and held that baby. Finally, about daybreak, the fever broke.

Morning came and with it the doctor. He said the baby had pneumonia and could possibly have died if we hadn't done the things we did. All we had had were a few hot onions and our faith in God, so I thanked God for that baby's life. I've often wondered about that couple and if they ever think of the little Appalachian girl who cried, walked the floor, and prayed with them all night long in that snow storm.

When we left Charlotte, I left kicking and screaming and clinging to friends I'd never forget. Virginia, Betty, Twiddle, Jack, Gene, and others. I'd always love them, and I thought my heart would break. I'd never recover. But being home in the valley with family and loved ones healed all the hurts.

It was good to hear the bells of old Mount Vernon Church again and to see cousin Fern. Fern and I again rode the Holston River in a rotten flat-bottom boat, went swimming in the deep hole, climbed Breakneck Ridge, and listened to the hounds run the knob after some fox that may or may not have been there.

Fern talked a lot about a young man named Walt Salyer, and I talked a lot about one named Feddie Fugate. Some Sundays we could walk from church with them under the stars. We walked the railroad track—one mile from home to church. The moon glittered showing the young men on one side of the track and us on the other.

Then Walt and Feddie went away to college, and the Carter sisters and Mother Maybelle moved away from the original Carter Family.

My Aunt Sara and Uncle A.P. were divorced in the late thirties, and even though they continued to work together, Aunt Sara married Coy Bays, father's first cousin. Uncle Coy and Aunt Sara decided to move to California, and Uncle A.P. took my cousin Joe and went back home to the valley. So in 1943 the Carter Sisters and Mother Maybelle moved to WRNL in Richmond, Virginia.

We would start a new show and a new kind of life together—just the four of us.

> Richmond girl, Richmond girl,
> You've got your golden tresses
> Twisted neatly into curls.
> The pride of the south is in you
> You queen of the Old Dominion,
> You're a proper southern lady,
> Richmond girl.
> —Johnny Cash

I still talked with a deep southern accent as a result of my years in southwestern Virginia, Texas, and North Carolina. I could never get the *out* or *house* out just like the people from the Tidewater area in east Virginia. When we moved to Richmond in 1943, I entered John Marshall High School and began to learn to be a Richmond girl. I said good-by to the girl in coveralls and billed cap. My days of logging were over. It was a time of growing up to be a cultured southern lady.

A Richmond girl learns to cut a French-style green bean. She learns to change the light, fluffy priscilla curtains for the heavy drapes in winter, to replace the straw mats with wool rugs, and to put on the linen slipcovers in the springtime.

And it was proper for a Richmond girl to know how to ride, so Helen and I went to the Richmond Riding Academy.

"Sure I can ride," I yelled as I leaped upon the back of that dark brown mare. Helen was taking it a little easier, a little scared but really excited. I had dreamed of how I'd look sailing over the hills clinging to the back of some sleek, beautiful animal, and now was my chance.

There were about five of us in all, along with the director of the academy. We walked our mounts out of the barn and went at a slow pace for a few hundred yards. The director didn't know that we really couldn't ride because Helen and I just hadn't told him. Besides, I had ridden those old "plugs" from the farms in the valley, and I knew I could do it. I had seen Gene Autry and Roy Rogers blazing the trails of the west, and I wanted to get on that mare and go.

Go I did. The horse was trained to run, so away we went. But things weren't as I had planned them. To begin with, the saddle had no horn. Old Roy's and Gene's saddles had horns, and I wondered what I was going to hold on to. All the dignity and gracefulness I had imagined seemed to fade away around the side of that horse. Because that's where I was at the time. Way around the side. I bumped there awhile trying to figure out how I was going to keep from falling off.

"Post! Post!" they screamed at me. Post—my foot. A post was something you strung wire to for the fence.

"It's all in your legs," they said. "You've got to sit, then stand in the saddle, English style." My dignified

English ancestors would have turned over in their graves. There I went—my feet straight out in the stirrups in the most undignified manner you could imagine. I had just learned that if I stood up, then sat down, at least I'd stay on top of the horse instead of around the side where I'd been hanging for the last fifteen minutes.

Then I heard the horn. I couldn't believe it. Across the road darted the dogs, the hunters after them, all following a fox, and my horse decided to get into the chase. Canter—canter. Since I'd only learned a minute ago how to keep from falling off, I decided the best thing for me to do was to hold on to the mane. Pray, post, and scream. I did all those very well. And all I could see was my very excited horse fast after the pack, with blue sky and sunshine between me and the saddle.

I never saw the fox, but it was the beginning of my love for riding. Helen fared much better than I, as she learned how to say "Whoa" first of all. That only came to me after a very scary ride and a very bruised bottom and legs.

Mother would come to the riding academy to pick us up. She'd sit in the car and wait for us, and it never dawned on me to ask her if she could ride until that day. . . .

Mother was waiting as usual, watching Helen and me riding around posting—all very proper—with our English riding boots and jodphurs. Then she spotted a big black stallion, the academy's best jumper and one I'd never dared to ride. She got out of the car, walked slowly toward that big stallion, walked around him, and just bounded upon his back and took off in a dead run.

I almost fainted. "Help, help!" wasn't good enough because there went my precious mother on the back of that wild horse, sailing over a fence jump before anyone could stop her. She took a couple more, rode him to a screeching halt, jumped off, and never even gave her two wobbly-kneed daughters a second look.

"He's a good jumper," she said calmly while I was screaming, "You could have been killed!" She just laughed and remarked that she'd ridden worse with a basket on each arm taking "dinner" to the sawmill crew back on Copper Creek.

To be a sponsor was the greatest thing that could happen to a high school girl in Richmond. The young men entered the Cadet Corps, drilled, learned military discipline, and looked for a young lady to be their sponsor and wear their colors and their captain's bars. To be a sponsor was my greatest ambition in my senior year at John Marshall High School. I wanted so to wear the colors of some handsome young captain and stand in line in review. I wanted the thrill of "eyes right" and all those handsome young men looking at me all at once, proud you were their sponsor, asking for advice and help, and accepting you as a friend.

Well, that's what I wanted, but getting it was another thing. Most of the captains already had girl friends, girls with beautiful shiny hair, stylish clothes, and sparkling personalities. I took a good look at myself. My hair went just where it wanted to go, and I was singing those hillbilly songs on that radio station every day and somewhere on a stage every night. I just didn't have the east Virginia "couth" those girls had. And I was doing that Aunt Polly Carter act. I had created a crazy country character called Aunt Polly Carter, who would do anything for a laugh. She wore a flat hat and pointed shoes and did all kinds of old vaudeville bits. A good captain sure wouldn't want his lady to be that silly.

But it meant so much to me that I just started praying about it. My best friend, Joyce Dobbins, was going to be a sponsor, and she prayed for me, too. I did learn that there was one young man who didn't have a sponsor yet—the First Battalion Commander, Bobby Spires. But he was so handsome, and I didn't even know him. It all seemed hopeless. But God did answer the prayer of a fifteen-year-old girl. That young captain marched right up to me on the front steps of John Marshall and asked me to be his sponsor.

What a wonderful year! My life style was different from most of the high school girls, but I stood just as proud when the boys passed in review with eyes right and broke into that old theme song of ours, "In the Blue Ridge Mountains of Virginia"—only we sang it, "We're the Carter Sisters from the mountains, and we're here to sing your favorite songs."

My prayer to be a sponsor was a small prayer, but my friend Joyce has since shared many a burden with me in prayer, and still does. She is a great Bible teacher and one of my dearest friends.

Mr. Troxall taught me to read notes that weren't shaped, and I sang in the girls' chorus and glee club. I stood as close to my friend June Bell as I could because she was always right on pitch. I was always standing close to someone who could sing right on pitch—it was handy.

I graduated from John Marshall in February 1946, and I cried because I wasn't going to college. Joyce and all my friends were going, and I couldn't understand why it was more important for me to work. But it was. Our family was a unit, and at that time they needed my part in the show. So we had our homemade college—the guitar, the songs, the road work, putting up public address systems, and the discipline of our parents. In the traveling we did I learned to sing all the parts, take up tickets at the door, drive all over the USA, and do what was necessary to make a good show.

Anita still stood on a chair to play that big bass fiddle, and she could yodel. I'd put my voice in there, but it just couldn't come through. The notes came out loud, high, and clear from Helen and Anita, so the more they sang on pitch, the crazier my routines became. We'd sing, do bits from vaudeville days, Anita would do her acrobatics, I'd do Aunt Polly, we'd have hymn time, I'd dance, Mother Maybelle would play her "Wildwood Flower," and our show sometimes ran two-and-a-half hours.

Richmond gave us five good years at WRNL, WRVA, and the Old Dominion Barn Dance. God was good to us and Mother, Helen, Anita, Daddy, and I were bound with a love you can't write on paper.

During the summer of 1946 we went home to southwestern Virginia. The valley never changed—it wasn't a changing place. But I had changed. I was a young woman.

The old circuits sometimes called for five shows a day. I learned to sleep in the car, get ready in five minutes, and tune a guitar in two. Sometimes I felt like I had little wool sweaters on my teeth. My body ached. Then I stopped a show with a routine, and I finally had to face it—I was hooked. There would be no turning back now. I would be an entertainer. My life would be different. I would not go to college, would not marry Feddie Fugate back home and raise children, cook three meals a day, and be an average American housewife.

Just before we left the valley for the first time when I was nine

When life was just four square miles

My grandmother, Mollie Carter, with cousin Joe and sister Helen

My sisters, Anita (left) and Helen (rig

With Anita (middle) and Helen (right)

Mother Maybelle, Aunt Sara, and Uncle A. P.—the original Carter Family

Left to right: Uncle A. P. and Aunt Sara, Mrs. Jimmy Rodgers, and my cousins Joe and Janette Carter

1946-47 at WRVA, Richmond, Virginia—when we had been broadcasting for eight years
Left to right: Helen, Anita, Mother, and I

My tomboy days—without the long-billed cap

My father, Ezra Carter, as a young man

I'm second from the left, wearing my captain's colors —my good friend Joyce Dobbins is fifth from the left

My friend Joyce today

High school days in Richmond

**GREETINGS FROM THE CARTER FAMILY
AND THE MAINERS**

Carter Family, Top Row: A. P. Carter, Janette, Brother Bill, Sara, Maybelle. Children: Helen, Aneta and June. The Mainers, Standing: Ollie and Zeke. Seated: J. E. Mainer and Price.

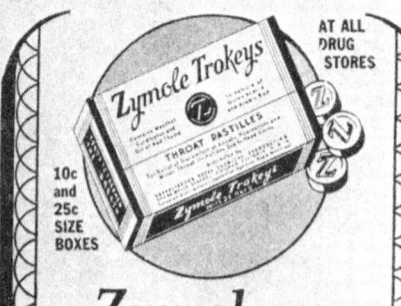

AT ALL DRUG STORES

10c and 25c SIZE BOXES

Zymole Trokeys

Fast, Quick Relief for Coughs Due to Colds, Smokers' Throat, Huskiness and Similar Throat Irritations

PATSY MONTANA and LITTLE BEVERLY

COWBOY SLIM RINEHART

Ambition

1950—when I first came to the Grand Ole Opry

Fabry, Nashville

His name was Chester Atkins, and I'd never seen anyone quite like him. He'd sit alone picking his guitar for hours. He'd only speak to you if you spoke to him, and he always sat in a little room just outside our dressing rooms in Knoxville, Tennessee. We were now a part of the Midday Merry-Go-Round, WNOX, with Lowell Blanchard, being heard in east Tennessee, North Carolina, and Kentucky. Chester was part of a group with Homer and Jethro.

How he could play—all those chords "around the corner"—and there I was still having trouble with my autoharp and the basic three. I had a desire to learn that fourth or fifth chord so I could play somewhere on the black notes, and I'd find myself listening to Chester play that guitar even more.

I buried Aunt Polly's silly hat and shoes and became plain old June Carter who would do anything for a laugh. But I was trying a little harder to learn how to play the guitar.

Chester came to work with us about 1947, so we now had my father and mother, Helen, Anita, Chester, the bass fiddle, and me all tucked inside our big Cadillac when we traveled. Chester became closer to us than a brother and was part of our show in Knoxville. Then he packed his car, his wife Leona, his daughter Merle, and away we went to Springfield, Missouri, to work at KWTO for another year.

When Chester was standing at the microphone playing the guitar, he would make some of the funniest faces I'd ever seen. But he was shy, and he would never talk on stage. I thought, if he could make that shyness work for himself, if he could convey his simplicity and warmth by just saying a few words, then along with his guitar playing, he would be a master communicator. So I vowed to do the impossible. I'd make Chester talk on stage.

I'd swing on the curtain way out over the audience just so Chester would tell me to stop it. Sometimes as he was playing his guitar, I'd run my nose up and down the frets—adding to or taking from whatever he was playing at the time. He had a vibrato on his guitar that looked like a gear shift, and I'd throw him into high or low whether he felt like it or not. And he gradually began to loosen up; he began to laugh.

Here I am bragging about how I taught Chester Atkins to talk on stage, when there is no way I can ever tell you what Chester meant to me and all of us and how much *he* taught us. He is one of the greatest guitar players in the world, and he was part of our family. He added to our lives and our show, and the quality of our music improved.

"You can't bring that guitar player with you," they told my father at WSM in Nashville.

"What do you mean?" asked Daddy. "If we can't bring our guitar player, then we just won't come." And that's how it would have been, too. They continued to call us daily from the Grand Ole Opry in Nashville, and they finally decided we could bring Chet Atkins with us. It wasn't because they thought he couldn't play his guitar. They knew he was probably the best in the business—and that was the trouble. The union musicians were afraid of the competition. Afraid he would soon take most of the recording sessions work away from them.

So they said we could bring him, but that he couldn't work with anyone except us for six months. Those were the union rules.

And it happened just that way. For six months Chet Atkins worked with us exclusively on the Grand Ole Opry and our early morning radio show. Then he did what they thought he'd do—he took all the business.

CHET

The hands of the baker
Or the candlestick maker
Are those of a skillful man.
The thread of the tailor
The ropes of the sailor
Are tied by knowing hands.

The watchmaker's eye
And a light to see by
And hands that are calm and sure
Make the tiniest springs
Do the finest things,
Long may the skill endure.

It matters not
The job you've got
As long as you do it well.
The things that were made
By plans well laid
The test of time will tell.

But how can you count
Or total the amount
Of the value of the man
By the melodies played
And the beauty made
By the touch of Chet Atkins' hands.

—Johnny Cash

It had a sound all its own—that radio show that aired every Saturday night over WSM in Nashville, Tennessee, or over NBC radio for one hour.

"Let her go, boys. This is the Solemn Ol' Judge, George D. Hay, in Nashville, Tennessee, at the Grand Ole Opry. Let her go, boys," he yelled. And on they came: the Fruit Jar Drinkers, the Gully Jumpers, Sam and Kirk McGee, Lew Childre, the string bands, and all kinds of people who just milled around backstage—two hundred or more there were, and the miracle was that no one got in anyone's way and everything went off as planned. It fit together like a jigsaw puzzle, some of the greatest pieces being the bands of Roy Acuff, Ernest Tubb, Eddy Arnold, and Bill Monroe.

Now our lives were to become part of this show that was the ultimate in country music, for in 1950 we came to the Opry, as did Hank Snow and Hank Williams, followed by Carl Smith, Webb Pierce, Faron Young, Cowboy Copas, and Little Jimmy Dickens. The 1950s in Nashville saw many a car—Lincoln or Cadillac—roll out headed in all directions over the United States, loaded with guitars, banjos, bass fiddles tied on top, feet and arms and legs stowed wherever they'd fit. And we were among them—the Carter Sisters and Mother Maybelle. Helen was married now and having babies, so we added Bea Puffenbarger as her replacement, then Becky Bowman.

Becky Bowman came in a 1947 Kaiser wearing a pair of anklets, a straight skirt, a pipe in her mouth, and about 160 pounds of smile. She was accompanied by a clarinet, a guitar, an accordion, a mandolin, a steel guitar, a bass fiddle, a long-billed cap, and a mother—Mama Bowman—and she smelled like Octagon tub soap.

The first words she ever said to me were, "I don't have enough hair to wad a shotgun," and she didn't. The little bit she did have had been blessed with a good old frizzled permanent, and it stood out in all directions. I looked at her in amazement, this girl from Kansas City, Missouri. I had seen her once before when we were all on a concert together in Kansas City when she was about twelve years old, and a lot of years had passed since then. Helen was having her second baby, so we needed a girl to sing Helen's part and play accordion.

Frankie Kay, a friend of mine from Kansas City, had said, "Becky Bowman might be able to do it. She can play anything else." So I had called Becky to come and take Helen's place. And here she stood.

I'll never forget the first time we sat down to rehearse. Becky picked up the bass fiddle and played all over that thing. She did wonders with guitar and mandolin and played the jazziest clarinet I'd heard. The accordion just sat in the corner, until finally I said, "Becky, I guess we'd better get down to these songs now with the accordion."

She picked it up, took a deep breath, and gave it a couple of yanks. Nothing happened. She just couldn't play it. She could play any other instrument—except the accordion. I had interviewed her; I had hired her. Now how was I to tell Mama that Becky couldn't play that accordion. Our whole singing routine was built around Helen taking the leads on the accordion. What was I going to do?

Well, I liked Becky so much I decided we would bluff it through, and we did. Becky's voice was fine, and

Mama still didn't know about the accordion. We went into the first morning radio show.

Becky put on her accordion, walked up to the mike with Anita, Mama and I, and belted out her good strong alto. Then Chet forgot to play the break that Helen always played! I looked at Becky and she looked at me. Then she took a deep gulp, looked to heaven, and—just played that accordion loud and clear—perfect.

She couldn't play one note on that thing in rehearsal, but when that little red light came on in the radio studio, it was as if someone pushed her button. She could play that accordion only in the studio.

I asked her later, "Becky, how long have you played that accordion?"

She said, "Well, I talked to you that day on the phone and went downtown and bought it."

Becky became my straight man, as Helen had been, and she moved into our home as part of our family. She became my dear friend for life and my sister in Christ, and my daughter, Rebecca Carlene, is named for her. She lives now in St. Joseph, Missouri, with her husband, Ed, and their daughters, Julan and Lorna.

The world we lived in then was so different than our world today—with airplanes, limousines, and one gigantic auditorium after another. Then we did not have the luxury of air-conditioned cars, and people often saw those Carter girls driving through the country in that long Lincoln with the windows open—Becky wearing her long-billed cap supporting a cold washcloth dangling in the breeze right in front of her nose—driving to make another show date after a Saturday night performance somewhere in Pennsylvania, Arkansas, or Texas. It was nothing to drive eight hundred miles during the night and play three to five shows the next day in an old vaudeville theater.

But I don't remember my mother ever complaining.

I always wondered how she did it. She'd hook that right thumb under that big bass string, and just like magic the other fingers moved fast like a threshing machine, always on the right strings, and out came the lead notes and the accompaniment at the same time. The left hand worked in perfect timing, and the frets seemed to pull those nimble fingers to the very place where they were supposed to be, and the guitar rang clear and sweet with a mellow touch that made you know it was Mother Maybelle Carter playing that guitar.

The Carter Scratch was probably developed out of sheer necessity, because in the old days when the Addingtons, Daughertys, Kilgores, Wamplers, and those wonderful people from the Copper Creek side of the mountain chose to have an all-night square dance, there just weren't enough musicians to make the sound the people wanted to hear. So mother took on the job of playing all the parts by herself, because they were lucky if they sometimes had a fiddle and my Uncle Doc Addington with his guitar and Uncle Duke with his banjo.

Those wonderful old English ballads that had survived the long boat trip over, survived the hot summers and cold winters, had come to be a part of my mother's heritage and her heart. And she held her autoharp with a delicate warmth and love that could never be duplicated and produced a light airy sound that drifted in with the soft motion of her hands.

There was no way I could play like my mother. I flung the picks hard at those strings—plucked, jumped, tore into that autoharp like I was driving a truck. But Mother was always gentle, always kind, and how she put up with us three girls never ceases to amaze me. The height of her anger was always a very special kind of tragic look that Helen, Anita, and I learned to regard with a quick respect.

We laughed a lot, sang a lot, and drove a lot. We girls sang new songs, but Mother continued to use the old Carter Family material, and we had a lively little show. It was a time when I did a lot of comedy and had a lot of ambition.

When I was young, I had ambition. Oh, I had such great ambition to be a funny girl. When I was ten years old, I met Cousin Minnie Pearl, famous for years as a comedienne at the Grand Ole Opry in Nashville, and she encouraged me. She said, "Always be yourself. Never try to copy or mimic anyone else. Be an individual." So I went home to the valley and started to live with my dreams of being a funny girl.

The week after I talked with her, Cousin Minnie sent me a letter and a lot of routines she had used on the Grand Ole Opry. That was the most wonderful thing that could happen to a little girl who had dreams of being a great entertainer. In the years that followed, I learned Minnie's routines, and I felt very special because she had taken the time to write to me when she was such a big Opry star. But I followed her advice, and I never used one of those routines. I developed my own.

I enjoyed several years of success as a funny girl, but somewhere in my heart there was always an empty place, and sometimes at night I would cry. I had fulfilled my ambition to be an entertainer, but somewhere inside there was still an emptiness. I didn't know what I was crying for.

There I was, performing every Saturday night at the Ryman Auditorium along with Hank Snow, Roy Acuff, Minnie Pearl, Hank Williams, Faron Young, Carl Smith, Webb Pierce, Uncle Dave Macon, Ernest Tubb, and Red Foley. I should have been content, but I wasn't. And what happens when you aren't content? You just keep trying for more and looking for something a little better.

Of all the Opry folk, I was most attracted to a young man named Carl Smith, a new Columbia artist. We fell in love and were married in 1952. Our daughter, Rebecca Carlene, was born in 1955.

There is no way to put a finger on why that marriage failed. Perhaps if I had remembered all God's promises and claimed them in my life, it would have been different. God's order to wives is an important part of a successful marriage, and I'm afraid I fell short of what a wife should be. I continued to work with my mother and sisters. Carl was going one way, and I was going another. If a wife expects to keep her husband, she must think first of God's order—be a helpmate and forsake mother and father.

When your heart's broken, you gather the pieces together, take your little girl, and catch a plane to New York City. When I went to New York, I thought I was the ugliest girl who ever lived. You feel that way when a marriage fails.

With the help of friends I entered the Neighborhood Playhouse on Third Avenue and started a new life style. When I was unhappiest about the breakup of my marriage, I found strength in working—speech, drama class, ballet—things a girl from the valley just had never been exposed to at all. I found a new form of self-expression in acting. Sandy Meisner, my drama coach, let me enter a professional class that summer because a friend of mine, Elia Kazan, had recommended me to him. I was to learn from Joel Grey, Robert Fuller, Barbara Bain, Julie Wilson, Tom Poston, Larry Storch, and Robert Carle. Rosemary Edelman, who was in my drama class, came to spend the night and stayed to spend two years sharing an apartment with me at 20 East 67th. A world of make-believe became reality.

Harry Kalchiem at the William Morris Agency became my godfather. He sent me to all the networks and the movie studios. I beat the pavement, walking and praying for a little opening into a world I'd only read about. I bluffed my way onto the Garry Moore Show, the Jackie Gleason Show, and the Jack Paar Show, where I did the only thing I knew—I told stories, sang, and danced.

For the first time in my life I began to realize that some people just did not believe in my precious Jesus Christ, but that I still loved them even if they didn't. Rosemary bowed her head in respect as I said the blessings at the table "in Jesus' name," and I loved her as a sister. We were totally different—an English girl from

Clinch Mountain, Virginia, and a Jewish girl from Beverly Hills, California.

I was sure Rosemary was a pauper from the way she talked. A year later when I went to Hollywood to make a Gunsmoke sequence and do two leads on the Jim Bowie Show, I met her family and learned her father was the famous Louis F. Edelman, producer for Warner Brothers movies; in television he was executive producer for Wyatt Earp, the Danny Thomas Show, the Big Valley, and many more.

Lou and Rita Edelman treated me like a daughter. They even gave me Rosemary's car to drive while I was in California. I discovered Lou had ridden the train through our little valley in Virginia selling movies to the coal fields, when movies were a new thing. Through my contact with those dear people, I developed a love for the Jewish people that continued to grow through the years. Now I call myself an ingrafted Jew because of Jesus Christ and His promise to the Gentiles.

Each Friday, Carlene and I would fly home to Nashville, I'd wave to Carl, let him see Carlene, play the Prince Albert Radio Show as a comic, and fly back to New York. If money ran low, I'd work a week doing country music shows. I paid my bills, studied, and grew as a person. It was a hard, heartbreaking time for me when I finally divorced Carl Smith.

Working alone can make a girl ambitious. The Carter Family had given me a lot of backbone because that's what they were, my backbone. Now I couldn't waltz through a show and lean on them. I had to work alone. But the shadow of my mother and sisters often held me up—and always will.

They continued working as a family, while I had this little act I built for myself, using local bands of some of the stars I worked with. Out of necessity I had to learn to play the guitar—not just play around with it, but be able to keep the band with me in the right time on anything from "Wildwood Flower" to "A Good Man Is Hard To Find." I played the autoharp and the banjo and was a lot like Becky Bowman with the banjo. I just couldn't play it except on stage. Any place else, my hand just froze on the strings. My comedy became serious business now, and I worked hard at it.

I was sent to a famous studio and was granted an interview with the head of the studio. He gave me three scenes to learn and set an appointment for the reading. I'd done many readings, and it did not occur to me that the time he'd given me—six o' clock at night—was unusual. So I learned the lines, excited because this looked like it could really be a break.

When I went for the reading, he was there all alone. No secretary, no assistant—just he and I. My readings were from the part of a prostitute or a very fast woman, and I wondered where the actor was who would play the opposite role. I finally realized that the studio boss intended to do the part himself.

I did the first scene, and he was impressed. Then I realized what he was trying to do. He was not intent on his part of the scene, but on a real-life scene with the two of us. He told me I could have a part in a new picture (he named the part and the film), that I had great talent, and that he would help me to develop it in the late evenings.

Well, all I can say is, "Hell hath no fury like a Virginia mountain girl who's been insulted." I think I kicked him in the shin and let him hear about a thousand words on "Who do you think you are? Do you think because I've got this southern accent that I'm stupid? Nothing would put me in your bed, and if this is Hollywood, you'll never see the likes of me on your screen. If that's how some girls become stars, I'll just never be one. . . ."

I ran home crying. Rosemary and Robert Carle, another friend and drama classmate, calmed me down, and Rosemary took the calls that continued to come for a week. I never went near that studio again, and Harry Kalchiem never let me go alone to another reading again. I began to remember how precious my Virginia home was, remembering that line from the Bible, "It's all vanity."

Colonel Tom Parker booked me some, and I worked with Elvis Presley and heard a lot from Elvis and his friend, Red West, about a young man named Johnny Cash. Finally on a weekend home in Nashville to play the Grand Ole Opry, I met Johnny Cash. I talked with him backstage, and the next Saturday he brought me a record of "Folsom Prison Blues" and "I Walk the Line," and I became a fan of his. He seemed like a special person, but he went one way and I went another.

I moved back to Nashville in 1957, and I met and married Rip Nix, a fine young man from Madison, Tennessee. We had a daughter, Rozanna Lea, and we tried hard to have a good marriage. But it seemed Rip and I came from two different worlds. After six years, that marriage also ended in divorce.

This was probably the lowest point in my life, and even now it is difficult for me to write down these facts. I still had all the Puritan upbringing from the valley in Virginia, and I had all kinds of guilt complexes about everything. I'd planned my life: I'd be married one time to one man and raise a family, and that was it. And here I was—I'd gone through two marriages. I couldn't hold my head up and look people in the face. I was so ashamed at having gotten a second divorce that I kept it a secret for a long time. My parents didn't even know Rip and I were separated until he'd been gone for two months.

PEACE OF MIND

O Lord, I guess it's over—
I'm as low as I can get
In the sackcloth and the ashes
My cheeks are soaking wet.
I've pulled my hair
And wrung my hands
And still no comfort came,
I'd like to get up from here
And find someone to blame.
I really can't be Jacob
Clinging to some feet
And fighting wings a-flapping,
Struggling while I weep.
I claim the right for peace of mind,
It may take all the night—
Angels and me upon the ground,
It's really quite a fight.

I always believed that if I tried to do what was right by my neighbor, I would finally have my heart's desire. I really only wanted to see over the mountain in the beginning—just to be a part of the world, to see a ship the size of the *Titanic* without just hearing Mother sing about it. I wanted to see people of other lands and know what they were like.

When I was living in the valley, I had only seen one black person. We used to go Gate City, and sometimes we'd drive near the depot and we'd see him. He looked just like anybody else except he was black.

I wanted to see the yellow people. I'd only read about them with their different eyes. The Indians, the red ones, were the enemy at the Gate City Theater, and Gene Autry and Roy Rogers always won the battles.

I wanted to cross the great Atlantic Ocean and the Pacific, go to Australia and see a koala bear.

Well, I finally saw the yellow people, the red people, the black people, and I crossed the oceans. I saw happy people and sad ones. But the horror of it all was that I also saw the starving ones, all around me. The red, the black, the yellow, the white—we're all alike. And we all get hungry. I don't remember anyone in the valley ever being hungry, but out in this world I had wanted to see so badly, there were millions starving. And there was no little valley for them, no place of refuge or sanctuary.

The big ships I saw weren't always clean, the men weren't always polite, and the women weren't always pure.

I began to wonder why I had wanted out of that valley so desperately. Desperate to sing, to dance, to be somebody famous, to shake a president's hand.

I got up early and went to bed late. Run—drive—push—shove. And why? Why did I do it all?

Why not cling to the simple way of life from that small

valley? Why not accept peace of mind and the only cure for heartache, hunger, or strife? The sure cure that only comes from totally trusting in Christ like a little child from the valley.

Why do we always climb that mountain until we stumble and fall over the top—make all the mistakes—pour out our hearts and souls—become sinful and lost in that desperate jungle of life? But something drives us on and we do it.

I've come a long way from that lonesome valley, and I've been lost in that jungle. And that's why I now cling to the basic things I was taught as a child back in Clinch Mountain. Because I've been over the mountain, and it's all vanity. I'm only what I am today because of what I was in the beginning.

I continued to work. I knew how much money I had to make each year to support myself and my Carlene and Rozanna, and I worked till I earned it. We lived in Madison, Tennessee, with a housekeeper named Christine Bilbry, one of my dearest friends.

Sometimes I worked with Ferlin Huskey. We once did a movie for Paramount Pictures called *Country Music Holiday*. Ferlin was a good entertainer with a big hit, "Gone," and my little act took on a bit of importance. I danced, sang—new songs and old songs of the Carter Family—did some corny routines, sang some more. I also did shows with Marty Robbins, Faron Young, George Jones, Buck Owens, Eddy Arnold, and Don Gibson.

I did midwest tours for my old friend Hap Peebles, or a special week of working just for the Corbin Boys in Lubbock, Texas, played a week for Cass Walker in Knoxville, television shows, personal appearances at used car lots and supermarkets—all kinds of ways to make a living.

Sometimes I'd drive for thousands of miles—alone or with special friends who'd share my trips, my work, and my worries. Micki Brooks, Connie Dickens, and Jan Howard all rode many miles with me. Audrey Williams, Hank's widow, and I did one tour and yodeled for thousands of miles. Unless you know the quality of both our voices, you just can't imagine the sound that came out of that Cadillac convertible. It was horrible. I think the rocks broke up on the side of the road. But it was some of the best fun I've ever had in my whole life.

That old Cadillac convertible was really something. A $5,000 car, and the doors wouldn't even open. I remember Connie Dickens and I having to crawl out the windows.

When I'd made enough money, I'd go home to my daughters. Carlene and Rosey took piano lessons, swam, and skated. I loved being their mother. They were beautiful little girls, and I tried to let them spend as much time as possible with their fathers.

WSM's 9th Annual Country Music Festival

1952—at Symphony Hall, Boston, Mass.
Left to right: Me, Mother, Anita, and Becky Bowman

Chet Atkins

With my daughters Carlene (left) and Rozanna (right)

Susan Jenkins

1956—when I met Johnny Cash for the first time, backstage at the Opry

1949—with Mother and Chester Atkins in Springfield

Publicity photo from the days when I was working on my own

Johnny Cash

Johnny Cash, when I first began working with him in 1961

MCA

In 1961 I started working with Johnny Cash. I think it was Saul Holiff, John's manager, who first booked me on the Johnny Cash Show. I had planned to work ten days a month to make a certain amount of money per year. That would give me twenty to twenty-one days at home with my girls. Saul told me that the Cash troupe worked ten days a month and would like to have me with them. I accepted the job. Now I could have time with Carlene and Rosey, and I would not have to book my own dates and worry about travel arrangements. I guess my comedy routines were an added dimension to Johnny Cash's show so he bought all the days I had to offer.

I remember the first time I pressed Johnny Cash's shirt. Patsy Cline and I were working the Cash show in Des Moines, Iowa. Everyone was concentrating on their own part of the show, and John was getting ready to go on stage. He was wearing a light lavender shirt, kind of pretty but horribly wrinkled. It hung limp and helpless, and it was on his back. There was Johnny Cash getting ready to go on stage, and I couldn't believe that shirt.

Patsy and I discussed it. I had just helped her press her dress, as I always carried a little travel iron. So I told John to give me his shirt. Gordon Terry brought me John's shirt and pants, and I pressed them. I got the wrinkles out of that old lavender shirt and gave those black pants a neat little crease. This was my start as a valet, a role I filled for several years. Through the years I've pressed clothes on ironing boards, on beds, on chairs, and somewhere in France I even ironed down on my knees on my old rabbit-hunting coat in a coal bin.

I was a little afraid of them all. I mean those four: Saul Holiff and the Tennessee Three—Marshall, Luther, and Fluke (W. S. Holland). I'd worked under my mother's arm for years, so to speak, and they were a bit wild and reckless. Oh, I don't mean liquor or women. I mean just "ornery" (as Grandma would say).

It was after a few months on the road with them that I got a knock on the door of my motel room one day in Charleston, South Carolina. It was John, and he asked me to sew up some pants and press them for him. Then those four all came waltzing into my room with confetti—boxes of it. They began throwing it everywhere. It was on the bed, in my hair, in the commode—everywhere. And their singing!

I was screaming, "How will I ever clean it up?" And Marshall said, "Don't worry. Don't worry," and in he came with a large, heavy-duty vacuum cleaner and proceeded to suck up the confetti—and the bed sheets and the clothes. Everything in the room was sucked into that contraption except me. The only thing that saved me was that they ran out of gas.

They continued to pull these pranks on me for two or three more tours. Finally I'd had enough. I decided if I was to work with this crew, I'd have to stand my ground. They were driving me crazy!

So I bit my lip, picked up an empty bottle (the dressing room I was using happened to be filled with empty bottles in crates), and threw it at Fluke. He dived under a table. I threw another one and another until I had Marshall, John, and Luther hiding and screaming for me to stop. I let all my frustrations go until we were ankle-deep in broken glass. And I made them all swear they'd never scare the daylights out of me again. They conceded defeat, and I officially became one of the boys.

I also learned that to have their respect, you went straight to your room after a show, you kept your mouth shut, and you kept a proper distance.

They all became like brothers, but Johnny Cash was always special. I remember telling him that he had no excuse for ever doing a bad show: he was an excellent entertainer, and he was a good man. God would permit him no excuses. God's hand was on him. It was just something I knew.

It was a terrible shock when I found out John was taking pills. He dropped a few in front of me in Macon, Georgia, one afternoon, and I could hardly believe it. I knew he didn't sleep much at night. You could hear him roaming around his room if you were anywhere near. I could remember how it had been with Hank Williams a few years before when Hank took so much medicine for his bad back, and how my sisters and I had worried about him.

But the show always had to go on, and ours did. And I found myself fighting hard with Johnny Cash. It was only later that I began to realize I was fighting him for his life.

Once we were in Albuquerque, New Mexico, and we were all in the car waiting for John. He just wouldn't come out of his room. He wouldn't get out of bed, and we were going to miss the show in El Paso. He must have had a bad night, and bed was the only sensible place to be, but I was raised with the instinct that the show must go on no matter what.

I looked at Marshall, Fluke, and Luther, gritted my teeth, went back in the motel, flung open his door, and hollered at the top of my lungs, "Lay there, star!"

He came out of that bed madder than I'd ever seen anyone. I ran for dear life, knowing I'd be fired. But Johnny was out of bed and grabbing his pants. I was embarrassed, scared, and fired, but we were on our way to the airport to catch the flight to El Paso.

I sat there knowing I'd never get to work with the group again—a girl just doesn't holler things like that at her boss—and trying to figure out how I'd get new booking dates for the months ahead.

Later at the airport, when I had my head in my coffee cup, Johnny handed me an Indian peace pipe he had gotten in the souvenir store, and we made El Paso on time.

Marshall, Luther, and Fluke had so much respect for Johnny that they would never challenge anything he said or did. I had respect for him, too, but as I began to see the pills hitting him harder and harder every day, I began to fight dirty. At times his life seemed so hopeless that I wanted to back away and run. But something I could not explain held me tighter than glue, and I could not let go.

There seemed to be an endless supply of pills. John always had them, and we'd make the first two or three days of a tour with him never sleeping at all; he roamed around all night after doing a show. Then came the sneaky ways I tried to help. I'd steal them and flush them down the commode! Marshall or Fluke wouldn't do it, but when I didn't know what else to do, I'd steal his hotel key, sneak in, and find them. That wasn't easy. He'd hide them in a sock or some other strange place. I could only look for them when he was asleep, and sometimes it took days just for him to go to sleep.

When he woke up, I'd tell him what I'd done and ask him to forgive me for not giving him the choice. Sometimes he'd be mad at me, but not for long, and we'd get a few more dates played before he'd figure out a way to get more pills.

After Carl Perkins joined us, we had a Dodge motor home which we traveled in sometimes. John had his sack of pills and Carl had his bottle—and I worried about both of them. It was a terrible way to live, and I could never have made it without the help of God. I begged, cried, demanded, hollered, prayed, humbled myself in front of God. He was the only help, because Johnny Cash sure was hooked, and I wanted so for him to be well. If all that energy could be harnessed for God, what a powerhouse of a man he would be.

But his only drive seemed to be to get more pills. And when he did, he'd just roam around until he collapsed somewhere. We never knew where he was.

By the time John chose to move to Nashville from California, the only peace of mind I ever had was when he went to my parents' home and stayed in a room they let him have. They treated him better than a son. He would have worn me out, but not my daddy. Daddy fed him country ham and biscuits, chicken and gravy, and prayed through it all. He never lost faith. Daddy just kept praying and claiming John for God.

John broke all the locks on my folks' home. He had a phobia about locked doors and snakes. Heaven help you if you stood between him and either of them.

I remember a time during the rough years when we were in concert in Duluth, Minnesota, and I knew what a troubled man Johnny Cash was. That night I watched him from my motel window as he walked along the shores of the lake. As the sun began to rise the next morning, I went to the window and could see him still walking, carrying a burden only he knew upon his shoulders. And so I prayed again that God would look down from heaven and continue to speak to this man and to give him the knowledge and wisdom to become the man Christ would have him be. That morning I wrote these "Words for the Devil."

You won't win, Devil!
You wear a crooked hat,
You hit me in the low spots,
But the Lord won't let you do that.
You crawl upon your belly,
And you sneak in like a snake
And wait there for the funeral
With me sitting at the wake.
Oh, I've fallen in your trap before,
When temptation was so high,
And I've hurt and sweat a lot
And let you fool me with your lies.
But the Lord says, "Seek ye first
  the Kingdom of God,"
And that's what I'm gonna do,
So all the sins you've piled on me
Will be added unto you.

I sometimes talked to John's mother and sister Reba, in California, trying to give them some hope. But I was a scared girl. I guess I was in love with John then, but I had two little girls I had to raise, and I was afraid to even ask him to my house for fear they might find out about the pills. I wanted so to help him, but I still had to protect my children. So there was only one thing to do—pray, believe, and claim God's promises. And we all did that.

There are so many things I could tell about those years—the sleepless nights in the apartment he shared with Waylon Jennings, the wrecks, the pain, the hurt. He should have died a thousand times from an overdose or a wreck. He could still do a good show, and the Johnny Cash watchers just watched to see when he would die. But God never let him go, and neither did I.

I think the time I came closest to giving up on John was one day when he had run his tractor into the lake, and our friend Dr. Nat Winston and I were both pacing around his big round bed. John had been high on pills for days, and he had just sailed over the cliff into the lake on that little tractor. There he lay in the bed, shivering and shaking, and we could still see the wheels of that upside-down tractor in the lake just below the home in the cove. And for once I didn't know where the strength would come from to continue. Nat and I had a long talk, and I went home.

I drove slowly into the driveway, and my father walked out to meet me.

"What's wrong?" he asked.

"It's John," I said. "He'll never make it. Nat says if someone doesn't stay with him for awhile, he'll never come out of it."

My daddy took a deep breath, looked me straight in the eye, and said, "Then what are you waiting for?"

"Me?" I said. "I can't go. What will the neighbors think? I can't leave the children either."

Daddy said, "We'll all go if we have to. I don't want to hear any more of this 'what will they think' mess. He's going to be all right, and your mother and I will help you."

So we went—my daddy, my mother, me, and our good friends, Brack and Anna Dixon. We took turns, two at a time, twenty-four hours a day. And Johnny Cash got better. I've thanked my father's memory many times for his faith in John and in the Lord and for renewing my own when I needed it so desperately.

Johnny Cash didn't die. With God's help he picked himself up off the bottom of life and fought the worst battle the devil had been in for a long time. Satan must have been scared to death. All that power that had worked for him turned and plowed straight into him with all its might. Now the fight was the other way around, and Satan tried all the angles. But the power of God gave John the strength he needed. He fought and he won, and he made it through our first concert in Hendersonville—our first concert there and John's first concert without pills. His strength grew and spread to Carl Perkins, and I saw Carl give up drinking and knew his wife's prayers were answered just as mine were.

OF JOHN
Dedicated to Marshall Grant After 20 Years

"He's a giant," someone said,
Two hundred twenty pounds of bone
   and bread
And eyes that look you in the face,
That don't hide the inside place to place.
He's like a cat that's on the prowl,
Who stalks a prey and takes a bow,
And sings his songs of good and truth
And holds on firmly to his youth.
He's father, husband, adviser, friend,
He lives within this world I'm in.
His jaw sets firmly on his face,
The lines and scars have been someplace,
For the man knows steel and what it is,
But friends, the steel wasn't always his.

The fire started years ago
With aching bones that hurt him so,
And hours of riding in the car,
And driving days that were too far,
And two friends close as brothers
   by his side
Who worked and sweated for the ride.
The guitar, bass, and voice so low
Had made a hit and let it go.
Success was always hanging round,
But the big man stumbled to the ground,
For deception came to have its fill
In the form of a dainty little pill
To pick him up and help him on,
For the shows they hurt him to the bone.
And higher and higher on he went
Till the body pained and curled and bent.
And a boom-chicka-boom filled the place,*

*Luther Perkins

And a strong man leaned upon a bass,**
A drum was added to the beat,***
The bass and drum they didn't cheat,
And a young girl came to pray and cry
For fear that the Man in Black would die.
Nightmares, shows and pills and booze
Can show what a man can lose.
The crowds they came and cried inside,
For Satan took a joyful ride.
The hits they came on and on,
And the friends they sang a mournful song
For life jumped and reared and trod,
And we laid boom-chicka-boom
   beneath the sod.

For twenty years the man leaned upon his bass,
The terror around took him every place,
But like a tree planted there,
He joined the girl within her prayers,
And when all the world said,
"The Man in Black is dead,"
The bass man shook his steely head
And fought and pulled and stood at his side—
"I'm not here just to take a ride.
This man is more than blood to me.
He'll get up again—you'll see."

So the Man in Black reached for the sky,
And the bass man lifted him up high,
And God reached down and did His thing,
And the Man in Black took to a wing.
So the man stands tall, a giant today,
And deception it has flown away,
And me, the wife, and children seven
Thank you, bass man, for a step to heaven.
Twenty years have come and gone,
And you've been there all along.

** *Marshall Grant*
*** *W. S. Holland*

The Johnny Cash
I knew about 1959

At Folsom Prison
Left to right: Marshall, Luther Perkins, and I

Judy Mock

One of our greatest joys was working with the Statler Brothers
Left to right: Phil, Lou, Don, Harold

About 1961

The Tennessee Three
Left to right: Marshall Grant, W. S. Holland, Bob Wootton

John and Carl Perkins on Glen Campbell's TV show

© by Jim Marshall

"Yes, I'll marry you." Out it came, loud and clear, because John really had asked me in front of 5,000 people in London, Ontario, that fall of 1967. There we all stood on that stage. He stopped the show, and out it came in front of Carl, Mother, Helen, and Anita. There stood Saul Holiff in his hometown not believing his ears. I turned to Marshall, to Luther, to Fluke, to the Statler Brothers. I wished he hadn't said it. I ignored him. I tried to sing a song, to hum, to change the subject. And he just kept looking at me, waiting for an answer.

I couldn't believe he had really done it. But when he wouldn't look the other way and insisted I answer him—I finally did. I said it in front of everybody, and I couldn't believe I had said "Yes."

Oh, I knew I loved Johnny Cash. I had loved him a long time. But who was I to make such a rash decision. There were too many people involved. But I had said yes, only listening to the wants of my heart and somehow praying for a miracle.

What would Carlene and Rosey say? What about all the guilt I carried because I had failed in a second marriage. What about his children—his parents—my parents—my work? Would he really stay off pills? What about our life together? Where would we live? What right did I have to be so selfish just because I loved him—to think I could marry him? Could I really depend on him? How would his parents and his daughters accept me? I had ignored all these questions and said a big, loud *yes*. Now what was I going to do? With all these questions running in my head, I really had to do some soul-searching of my own.

Afterwards, Dr. Nat Winston said, "June, I know John has had a pill problem, and I believe he's whipped it. But what about you? Have you whipped your problem?"

My problem? I thought. *What problem? I don't have a problem.*

"You're too independent," he said. "If you want your marriage to work, you're going to have to do some switching of your priorities."

As the days went by, I began to see what Doctor Nat meant. So I made a few decisions of my own.

I would starve, but I would starve by Johnny Cash.

I would no longer lead. He would make the decisions, and I would follow him. Mistakes or trials—we would face them all together.

I tried to show John that whether he continued to be straight or not was his decision, not mine. I could only love him and hurt and cry if he failed. It was up to him, but I would be beside him depending on him in every way.

Then I really began to change as a person. I knew I had really begun to change the day I signed my resignation letter for the Grand Ole Opry after being there for seventeen years. There had been security in being with the Opry, but from now on my security would come from God and Johnny Cash. I sent John a copy of the letter.

I began to learn not to be so particular, such a perfectionist. Everything in the house did not have to be in place. Books could be strewn around the way Daddy liked them, instead of on the shelf. Other people could do some of the things I had always done for myself. I learned to devote more of my time to those I loved rather than to a demanding world outside.

And as John's respect for himself grew, so did my respect for him. We began to grow together.

In the years that I had worked with Johnny Cash, he had never been to my house more than two or three times. I was always afraid Carlene or Rosey would know he was taking pills, so I was afraid to have him come there. But as he improved, he began to get to know my children, and they grew to love him.

All those questions I had asked began to be answered. It was all right with his parents and mine. I would only work if he wanted me to. He would pay the bills when we married. Carlene, Rosey, and I would move to his house out on the lake. I would do everything I could to help him. And God took care of my guilt about the past.

After that famous proposal he made to me right on the stage in London, we talked it over and agreed we would marry in June. So we told Carlene and Rosey on a Tuesday night.

Carlene asked, "Why are you waiting?"

"Your school," I said. "You should finish where you're going."

She replied, "You could get married in Franklin, Kentucky, in three days."

And so we did—on March 1, 1968. Friday we spent our honeymoon in John's house, and on Monday Carlene and Rosey started school in Hendersonville.

It was beautiful out at that house on the lake with the spiders, snakes, rocks, glass, logs, and the warmth of our hearts.

I used to call the French Colonial house where Rosey, Carlene, and I lived "the golden powder puff"—it gave you that kind of feeling, with everything exactly in place. When we took only our suitcases and moved to the house of gray on the lake—with John—I had a mixture of emotions.

> I live within this house of gray,
> All stone and glass and wood.
> Though there are snakes and spiders,
> Crickets and snails,
> I wouldn't kill them if I could.
> 'Cause I lived once on a powder puff
> All gold and shiny white,
> Not even a fly or little ant
> Ever made it out at night.
> But God's hand rests on
>   this house of gray,
> We're in out of the cold.
> And the insects they live and reproduce,
> But the powder puff's too old.

I married Johnny Cash with no regrets, no looking back. I was no longer afraid to be happy. I had repented. God had forgiven me through the grace of Jesus Christ, and I would no longer carry that guilt. I could not change the past, so God cleared it all away and gave me a promise that I was His child.

My heart doesn't hurt any more. There is no more emptiness, and I would say I have been truly liberated. Sometimes I look around me now and see girls who are eaten up with ambition, who have no peace of mind, and they remind me of me before my complete dependence on God and before my happiness with my husband and my family.

People ask me, "How can you claim to know God the way you do when you've been married three times?"

It's because of the forgiving grace of God and because of Jesus Christ that I can claim the promise He gave me. Because of the love of Christ and His death on the cross, this sinner claimed His promise, was forgiven, and is a child of God.

If I had had the faith and commitment in the beginning, I could probably have saved my first marriage. It wasn't that I didn't believe in God, because I have believed in Him since I was a child. It was because I did not ask His help when I needed it so desperately. I did not depend on Him and let Him lead. I tried to do it myself.

The Christian church has always forgiven murderers, thieves, and other sinners, but just couldn't find it in their hearts to forgive the terrible sin of divorce. Divorce was high on the scale of unforgivables, somewhere way up there out of sight. And if you had to live through it, you also lived with the terrible guilt that was a part of it all. We Christians cannot ignore it any more; there are millions of divorces in the world today, and unfortunately many of them involve Christian brothers and sisters.

I feel such sadness when I see how easy it is to obtain a divorce these days. In years past, people stayed married because of guilt, because of hundreds of years of tradition—for many reasons. But the main thing was that they stayed married.

But can we condemn them all. They can't restore that broken marriage if they've destroyed it—it's gone. They can't go back.

There are those in the Christian church who will never forgive me for those broken marriages. But Christ died for people like me. People who mess up their lives and stand shaking in their boots with guilt, wondering if they're really going straight to hell. But He tells us to repent, and if we really do this and know in our hearts that He has forgiven us, then the sin is no longer ours. That's what I did. And if people cannot forgive me, they must answer for that. Please remember—we are justified in Jesus when we believe, but it can take a long time to be sanctified.

So I gave it to God, and He helped me. Christ now carries that great burden that almost broke my heart, and I know that the same thing will never happen to me again, because I ask Him daily to direct my steps and look to Him for the help I need in sorting out my life.

In the beginning, I'd have never believed I would eventually be married to Johnny Cash. Certainly it wasn't part of my plan. But as I look back over my life, I can see how God took my sins and mistakes and turned them into something good. I believe my life was pre-destined, pre-ordained, and I feel that God must have known about it all the time. The love that John and I share with our love for Christ is one of the most precious gifts God could have given us.

This poem is the only way I can express my feelings about my first two marriages and my life now.

THE BURIAL

Have you ever been to a funeral where they lay a body down?
They take someone who died and put him in the ground,
The people cry and pray and sing and stand about for hours
And put in earth and pat it down and then cover it up with flowers.
It's too late once he's in the ground; you won't see him again,
And there's no way to alter things or change what they have been.
I've been to lots of those; I've seen friends and relatives put away dead,
But let me tell you about two burials of men that I have wed.

About the first one, a fine young man, handsome and with some wealth,
I'd never heard of sin; I was pure as nature's health.
I trusted in my first love and followed him about,
But he was young and reckless and his love it soon burned out.
I took him to the graveyard, quiet and silent near a tree,
And there I mourned his passing—there was no one there but me,
For his body went on living, walking out about the town,
But in my soul he died then,
So I slowly put him down.

Then there came another man, not really from my world.
He said he'd look out after me, me and my little girl,
And I had just come home from the wake and didn't see things too clear,
But I knew now what sin was and was covered up with fear.
A big mistake which was hard on my puritan soul,
So I wept and mourned and went back again to dig another hole.

I finally found the right man; he's been my lover, pal, and friend.
I won't have another burial, no, I won't do that again.
If I go back to that graveyard, there'll be friends and flowers around,
There'll be singing, mourning, wailing, and it'll be me they're putting in the ground.

I resolved to be a good wife for John. Steel is strong because it knows the hammer and white heat. Surely I must be forged into steel by now. I would try God's order, written in His Word, and would make an honest effort to be a dependent wife. I would look to John as the head of our home. I would be his helpmate. He would make the decisions, and I would throw away all that old independence I'd known for years. If we were poor, we'd be poor together. If God blessed us, we'd be blessed together.

When I married John, I'd already learned to love his children—Rosanne, Kathy, Cindy, and Tara—and our children had wonderful times together. God helped us grow as a family and taught us to grow in the Word and the Spirit.

John and I never left each other's sight for a full year. This was a vow we made to help protect us both.

Earlier I mentioned that I had always had great ambition. Now I began to realize just how dangerous ambition can be, especially for a wife and mother. There is only one way to be happy—put God first in your life. He has laid down a plan for woman that is a sure way for happiness—God first, husband second, and children next. A young wife eaten up with ambition can easily lose this order of things. I speak with authority on this subject, because that is exactly what I did. But through prayer and faith and finally a total commitment to God, I found out that ambition is all vanity.

He says, "Seek ye first the kingdom of God and all these things will be added unto you." Now, the greatest thing in my life is being a wife and mother and a helpmate to my husband. A woman is truly liberated when she gets these things into perspective.

There is nothing quite so thrilling as being on that stage and singing a song with John and being part of his life in every way. But God is first, John second, and third is the sacred trust of raising our children.

I haven't stopped to think about the old ambition in years, and the emptiness is gone.

TO JOHN

I try to remember the things that are precious to you,
And I'd give you money if that would do,
But money won't do it—that's not your way,
Your money's been for giving away.
Now if you precede me and go to your grave
And the angels knock the clouds about when Jesus comes to save,
I'll be standing there to rise with you
And to go up as you do.

And I will always love you, you'll always be mine,
Forever and always till the end of time,
Till the mountains split open with the weight of the sun,
We'll rise up together . . . as one.

So I'll let my hair hang down
'Cause that's the way you like it,
And I'll keep myself neat and nice for you,
And I'll have good food on your table,
And I will keep your house in order.

And I will always love you, you'll always be mine,
Forever and always till the end of time,
Till the mountains split open with the weight of the sun,
We'll rise up together . . . as one.

And I will pray for you, for your wisdom
And understanding and your charity,
And even if you've been wrong, and I've known it,
You've always been right,
Because that's God's order.

And I will always love you, you'll always be mine,
Forever and always till the end of time,
Till the mountains split open with the weight of the sun,
We'll rise up together . . . as one.

And I will smile for you and I'll be kind,
And I'll love your babies just as I've loved mine,
And when I could give you nothing,
God blessed me and I gave you a son.

And I will always love you, you'll always be mine,
Forever and always till the end of time,
Till the mountains split open with the weight of the sun,
We'll rise up together . . . as one.

The house of grey on the lake

1970—John with his parents and brothers and sisters
Left to right: Roy, Louise, John, Reba, Joanne, Tommy
Seated: Mr. and Mrs. Ray Cash

OUR WEDDING
Left to right: Rosey, Carlene, Micki Brooks, and Merle Kilgore

Left to right: W. S. and Joyce Holland, Marshall and Etta Grant,
Luther and Margie Perkins

"Going to Jackson"

John isn't always pretty

1976—John had me revive Aunt Polly Carter

House of Cash, Hendersonville, Tenn., our offices and recording studio

1969—on Vietnam tour, signing autographs for the servicemen

John and I relax with our good friends, Ruth and Billy Graham

Home & Children

J. T. Phillips

Although your life style may differ from mine, the basics are the same. You still have to cook the meals, scrub the floors, and care for the children.

The size of the house does not make the home. You can live in dignity and grace in a one-room apartment.

❦

There are so many things that contribute to my happiness at home with my husband, and here are some that are important areas to me in daily home life.

Homemaking is important to me—in my person and in my household. I always try to have on a clean, fresh dress at dinner in the evenings and to keep my house in order. I am a good housekeeper, but I also think sometimes you have to live with good clean dirt. I believe a house should be lived in and not just looked at. There are no forbidden areas in our home. It is all for living and the pleasure of the family, and I try to make every little corner a place where there's comfort. Children should feel "at home" in their home.

I do not mind cooking and scrubbing, but I find that I don't have time to do all of that any more, so it's my responsibility as a wife to see that it's done properly. Any man loves a clean pillow for his head at night.

Well-planned meals are essential. I try to have enough food for dinner in case John chooses to bring home a few guests, and I encourage the children to bring their friends. I've always said to John, "Just give me fifteen minutes." I'm reminded of the time he told me we'd have twenty-four people for lunch; I had to do some fast running to figure out how we'd finally feed those seventy-six who came. But I don't think anyone went away hungry.

I love a beautiful table. I have many sets of old china, linens, and silver, and I use them all. I don't put away my good things for Sundays, but use them every day. I like fresh flowers on the table and thoughout my house. Things I don't like are milk cartons or salt boxes on the table. I think a meal should be served with a little dignity, even in the poorest and simplest of circumstances. Order and neatness aid in good digestion and good health.

We raise our own beef and slaughter our own meat. I'm afraid of some of the preservatives in foods today, so I feel good knowing where our meat comes from. Because we feed so many people, I keep five freezers stocked as well as possible. We go to the store about once a month. That saves time and money.

It's a pleasure to serve the vegetables raised in our own garden. John, John Carter, and George T., Kelley's husband, always put out a beautiful garden, and we try to freeze all the excess vegetables for the winter's use.

It's good to be able to have a *family worship* time, but because we travel so much, we don't always do this. So when we bless our food, we often pray about some of our family problems. It's a good time, while getting the food blessed, to include friends, letting them know you care about their personal problems. Around the dinner table is a good place for worship and praise. If you find it difficult to get all you family together for prayer, try the table. They'll never miss a meal, and soon they'll look forward to this time of just praying together—not just about food, but about thanks and worship. Love for God sometimes takes on new meaning in this atmosphere.

I believe in having prayer with my household staff. This strengthens our home and our staff as well as myself.

A *kind, gentle manner* is something I have always desired. If you have a temper, try this. Always give thanks to God in all things. If you are so angry at you husband that you can't stand the sight of him, get alone—or pray silently—and say over and over, "Praise God, and thank You, God." And if it takes the anger to bring praise to God through your lips, it's all worth it. Say it over and over—"Thank You, Jesus"—and raise your right hand to God (you're closer that way). Say "Thank You, Jesus" until you finally feel the comfort run down your arm. Then the anger actually disappears, no matter what your problem. If you are hurt, disappointed, worried, jealous—whatever the problem—give thanks for it and He will help you bear it. Get yourself right with Him, and He will give you the kind gentle manner that establishes good self-control so needed in a marriage.

It's hard for a husband to continue to be mad at you if you aren't throwing harsh words back at him. A sweet smile and a word of encouragement could easily turn the tide.

I can remember thinking that *sex* must be a dirty three-letter word. But an attitude like that is a hindrance to a good marriage. Sex is to be enjoyed and to perpetuate the human race. It should not be put on a high spiritual level—it is to be enjoyed as God meant it to be. He gave us these human feelings and emotions, and we shouldn't be ashamed of them. Sex is an important part of marriage.

One of the hardest things I had to learn was that I could not do everything myself. I wanted to scrub all the floors, wash all the windows, wash all the clothes, iron them, be wife to John, be mother to our children, write songs, sing on the stage, see all those people, take care of all that business, tune that guitar, strum that autoharp. But there was no day long enough to get it all done. So I started praying for help. It was just more than I could do alone. My back hurt all the time, and my mind wouldn't let me rest when I'd lie down to sleep. I had to raise my right hand many times to overcome on this one, but God worked it out for me and sent some great help:

Reba, John's sister, who helps me with the business end of things—she is manager of House of Cash, our offices—will tackle anything (even scrubbing, if that's what it takes).

Dora and Sonny Franklin from Gallatin—Dora cooks our meals, and Sonny helps with just about anything that needs doing in the house.

Anna and Armando Bisceglia, born in Naples, Italy, live nearby. Armando's our head security guard, and Anna helps me whenever I need her—anything from baking zucchini Italian-style to putting out fresh towels for a guest.

Letha Barksdale who helps with the cooking and the laundry sings great and prays a beautiful prayer.

Virgil Morrow, our gardener, who helps me grow all those beautiful flowers I love to have for the house. He cares for my rose garden, my very special prayer garden.

These are all good Christian people, and we're all striving together for the same thing, the glorification of our Lord, Jesus Christ.

We sometimes entertain friends and business associates together at our home. I believe in having plenty of food and just enjoying the good company. Sometimes these parties may grow to 150 or 200 people. It's better to have about 100, because I can get that many in my lakeside living room if we're sitting people to people.

There we mix the new young writers and our old friends together and just sing for hours.

Before I had a cook to help me, my mother, Helen, Anita, Reba, and friends Micki Brooks, Anna Dixon, Jan Howard, and Mildred Joyner would help me out by bringing special dishes of their own. It was a great way to carry on the tradition of "dinner on the ground"—on my dining room table.

How can we say "You can't do that" when they've done it? Or, "You're not big enough." Of course they are, if it's done already.

We can teach our children what is right and what is wrong, but there comes a time when they must make their own decisions. They must make their own mistakes. And Mama can't do it for them. It's hard to let go, and we're tempted to say, "Where have you been? What did you do?" And most of the time we do. It's hard to trust, even when we know we should.

I weep for the frustrations of my growing children, but they must suffer their own mistakes and despair. It would be so easy to say, "Don't make that mistake, because I made that same one twenty years ago. And if you'll listen to me, I can save you all the trouble you'll face. Turn the other way." But we can't do that! Our children have their own lives to lead. The only thing we can do is commit them to God, asking Him to bring their lives into His own order and make them stronger by their mistakes. We must praise God for them on our knees.

I give myself these guidelines to live by for Christian family living:

The Word of God and its order—God, husband, children
Self-control
Prayer
Love
Listen
Understanding
Charity
Give attention to little things
Read to the children
Commit my family to God, believing in His promise

And I *thank God daily* for our children:

I thank God for warm, gentle Tara—for her beauty, her grace, and her love for God.

I thank God for sweet Kathy—for her bubbling laugh, her infectious manner, and the good mother she is for Thomas Gabriel.

I thank God for Rosanne—who has become so much a part of me that John Carter thinks "she came out of Momma's tummy too."

I thank God for Carlene—for her stately beauty, for her music ability, and for the way she cares for her children, Tiffany and John Jackson.

I thank God for Cindy—for her beautiful long black hair, her dark eyes, the way she glides through a room.*

And I thank God for Rosey—for those big eyes, that personality that makes all her sisters want to sleep in her room with her, her hard times, her triumphs, and her love for Momma.

And I thank God for John Carter's life.

Whoops! Just had a new granddaughter—Cindy gave birth to Jessica Brock—and she looks like her Grandfather John!

FIRST DATE

"Oh, run and get your boots,
Also your coat and hat,
It's snowing hard and icicles form
And you can't go out like that.
You've got to cover up real good
Or you might get the croup.
There'd be no way to thaw you out,
Not even with hot soup."

It's her first date, and he hit the horn
And she headed for the car
In silver slippers, cotton dress,
And she left the door ajar.
At fourteen years she's real mature,
I hope she stands the test
To say the things that she should say
And stay one of the best.
But rest assured, she'll never freeze,
Her heart is running warm.
God'll put His arms around her
And keep her safe from harm.
And I know where there're boots
  and coats
And warm things covered up with fur—
At home and in her closet
And not a one on her.

It scared me half to death
To let her have that first date,
So I went and hid behind the curtain
And decided it was there I would wait.
But when she came in at ten o'clock,
I'd said my prayers again,
And God gave me the wisdom
Not to ask her where she'd been.

It would be wonderful to always keep your girls at home, but girls will grow up and leave you with an aching heart and an empty room. All six of our girls are away now: Carlene, Rosey, and Rosanne are all singing and trying to have a career; Kathy and Cindy are taking care of homes and their children; and Tara is finishing her high school in California. This little poem is for all of them.

Pick up your clothes
Wash your tub
Try to do a little better.
Dust your dresser
Straighten your bed
Please fold up that sweater.

Your room is clean and empty
It's dusted where I've trod,
Your clothes aren't strung
   from east to west,
They're in the closet on a rod.

But I'd welcome your lovely
   laughter
And the sound of your guitar
And your clothes from floor
   to ceiling
And papers scattered far.

For loving you is easy,
And gosh I miss you so,
I'd gladly pick your things up
If you'd just never go.

Tara Cash

Cindy Cash Brock

Kathleen Cash Brimm

Carlene Carter

Rosanne Cash

Hope Powell

Rosey Nix

"It's a boy, June! Can you hear me? It's a boy!"

"He's kinda red all over."

"Do you think his head's all right? Let me see his feet."

"He's got my hair. Oh, my goodness, he looks more like me than you!"

Here I'd had all these visions about this little baby boy I was going to have. He was going to look just like his daddy. He would run around with his black mass of hair on his head and would look just like John. But that wasn't so. There he was—the first time I'd seen my newborn son, and he looked just like me. Only I wanted his little face to have those strong Johnny Cash lines, and I couldn't tell if he had them or not because he was so small, red, swollen, and crying.

John Carter Cash had arrived, and I was so proud to be his mother. And his father was proud, proud to have a son. Oh, thank You, God.

I couldn't believe the flowers—they were everywhere, from floor to ceiling in that big hospital room and out in the hall, even at the nurses' station. And the letters and telegrams! From governors and the president and people all over the world—wiring and writing and calling to say how truly glad they were that John had a son. I sent 2,000 thank-you notes for presents and could not believe how happy everyone was for John.

On his weekly television show for ABC, John said, "Hello, I'm John Carter Cash's daddy."

A woman is conditioned for nine months for the birth of her baby, and one of the greatest joys during that time is knowing that that baby has been conceived in love and anticipated with joy.

Winifred Kelley, a special duty nurse, tried to be sure I ate the right things to make good milk. She took such an interest in looking after me and my baby that I asked her to help me find a good nurse to travel with us and help us care for John Carter. She said she would try.

John Carter Cash came home to sleep in a bassinette by my bed, and we went through all those little goodies parents do: I walked the floor. John walked the floor. We wore out two grandmothers, friends, and me again because John Carter suffered some from the colic—especially late at night. But these were the things that made it all special. And our girls loved him very much.

I was trying to begin working again with John on the TV show and the concerts, but I was concerned about being able to perform and still care for John Carter. Then Winifred Kelley decided, after twenty-one years at Madison Hospital, that she would take the job of being John Carter's nurse. I had prayed that God would send me a good woman to help me be a wife and mother as well as a performer, and He sent Winifred. She came with the blessings of her husband, George T., and the five Kelley children—and a prayer to God that we would have more to say to the world than just to sing songs. Kelley and I shared our love for Christ together, and we were bound with that love only Christians understand.

At first I carried John Carter in my arms, then on a little carrier. I had to learn how to catch airplanes on time, figure out some private place to nurse my baby—with Penni Lane, my hairdresser, combing my hair and Jo Coulter putting on my make-up—all at the same time, check in and out of hotels, wash baby clothes—because baby things need to be fresh—be a wife, a mother to the girls, and still get in "Jackson" with John on the stage. With Kelley's help it all worked. Even the TV shows.

John Carter would ride on the front of my arm going everywhere. To Australia, Tasmania, New Zealand, Europe seven or eight times, to Israel to do *Gospel Road*. He went every place we went. He learned all the zoos in the world, the museums, and learned the stories of the Bible from John and I or Kelley.

I wanted him to know about nature, hoping that through it he could see God clearer in his young mind. I wanted him to know about animals—chickens, horses, cows—to gather eggs, and to work in the garden. So we bought a farm, and with the help of George T., John Carter has become a good country boy. He works planting seeds, growing his own things.

I've watched John Carter grow into a handsome little boy. But he's not too good yet to get a little paddling. I'll admit we do more talking than whipping, but he really minds good. And it's encouraging when Rosey comes home and says, "Mama, I'm so glad John Carter's not spoiled." He goes on stage sometimes if he chooses, and if not he plays. He makes up his own songs and puppet shows. He loves show business, but says he'll be a magician or a puppeteer, and sometimes his shows are better than ours I do believe.

Since he was born, every day I've held him in my arms and said, "Mama loves her little son." One of my most joyful moments came during a ride between Reno and Lake Tahoe when John Carter, who could hardly talk yet, looked at me and said, *"Son loves his little mama."*

We had gone to the farm without John Carter. That was something we had never done, but we were visiting with Anita and Bob Wootton at their farm near ours, and we were looking for some land.

We got a call at the home of Jean and Luther Fleanor,

our farm manager, and I saw John's face go white. There had been a jeep accident. The doctor said they were all hurt—Reba, John Carter, Cousin Kevin, Cousin Kelley, Timmy, Loney and Joannie Hutchins, and John Carter was hurt the worst. We were finally told he had a 50-50 chance to live.

John and I prayed all the way to Nashville, kneeling on the floorboard of the car. Bob was driving, and John was asking God to send the angels to minister to our little boy. I was praising God—but it was the hardest thing I ever had to do. That two-hour ride was a nightmare. When we reached Madison Hospital, there was Grandma Cash, Doctor Isaeff, Doctor Billy Burks, and Roy and Barbara Orbison, our neighbors. Doctor Billy said, "He's all right. I heard him cry."

But John Carter wasn't there. They had taken him to Vanderbilt, so I knew his skull must be fractured. When we got to Vanderbilt, there was Rosanne with her Bible. I could see our friends—Kris Kristofferson, Vince Matthews, Larry Gatlin—and the cameras. I thought I would die.

But God was so good to us. In the emergency room, we saw him. I said, "Son, it's Mama. Do you know me?" He raised his little hand and cried. Then he was unconscious again. So we all went upstairs to pray, and God did answer our prayers.

God took care of all the others in the accident, and they recovered, and John Carter only had three stitches in his head. I looked around me at Roy Orbison, who stayed to pray with us; he had lost his own two boys in a fire. I saw my sister Helen, who had lost her son Kenny in an accident when he was fifteen. I saw Grandma Cash, who had lost her son Jack. I praised God and thanked Him for these dear people.

Five days later we took John Carter home.

INTENSIVE CARE

You can't move me from this door,
I'm clinging, hanging on the floor.
That's my little boy inside,
He's hurt and lifeless from a ride.
The sign says "Intensive Care,"
I see knees and feet and hear voices there—
"Please move, ma'am, you can't stay here
   and pray,
You'll have to get up and go away"—
But I'll tell you, ma'am, there's just no hurry,
'Cause if I move, it'll be me you'll bury.

For seventeen hours I watched the lifeless
   little form,
And God was good, I heard him cry,
Just like when he was born.
But, God, I think he looked up first at You,
And came on back to help his mom and dad
To finally see them through,
Came to take another look at things,
When we knew he'd almost gone.
And we thanked God and we praised Him
And then we took John Carter home.

A LESSON FOR JOHN CARTER

I wanted my little boy to know
About the river, rain and snow,
The changing seasons all around,
About the planes, the boats, the towns,
But most of all I hoped that he
   could have a barn,
Not a fancy one with charm,
But an old loft all full of hay
With white doves who could get away
But chose to stay because
They liked the horse and chicken noise.
He'd gather eggs all blue and green,
The strangest eggs you've ever seen,
And have a sheep that just followed
   the goats—
The goats are the ones who stand
   and gloat.
Old Spotlight has fathered all the herd,
All are nannies, that's the word
From George T., who is boss and friend
Of John Carter, cow and horse and hen.
There are kindergartens, prep schools,
   and such
To give a young man just the touch
To get in to Harvard or Yale,
But understanding and common sense,
   I think they tell the tale.
And if there's danger of a young man
   getting stuck up,
There's a sure cure—
Just let him shovel some plain old
   chicken manure.

Bill Goodman

Baby shower for John Carter

Left to right: Edyth Cothren (her husband is the doctor who delivered John Carter), Reba, me, Elizabeth Cothren, and Micki Brooks

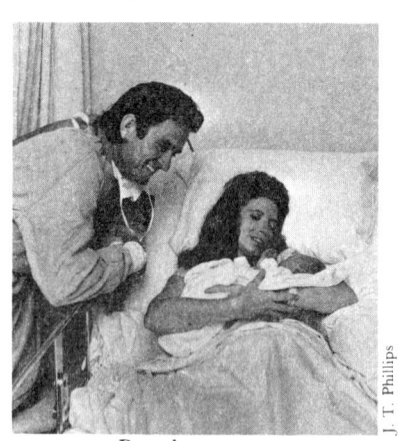

Proud parents

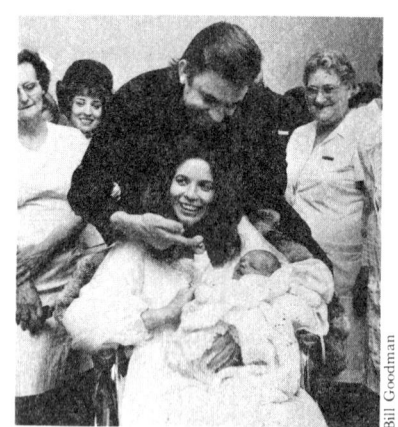

J. T. Phillips

Going home

Bill Goodman

On tour in Sweden

n Persson

On stage in New Zealand

Las Vegas News Bureau

n Carter's first birthday, when he
sented the Madison Hospital with
layroom for the pediatrics ward

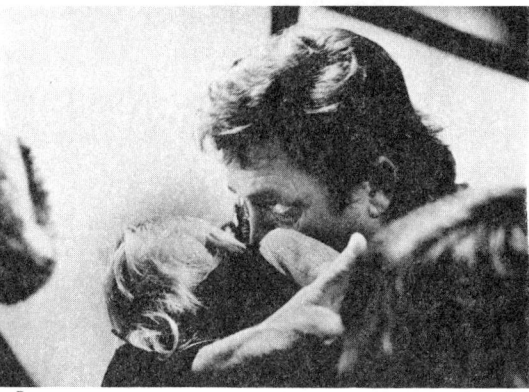

Jan Persson

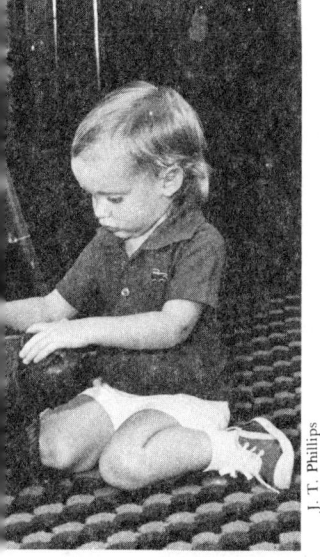

J. T. Phillips

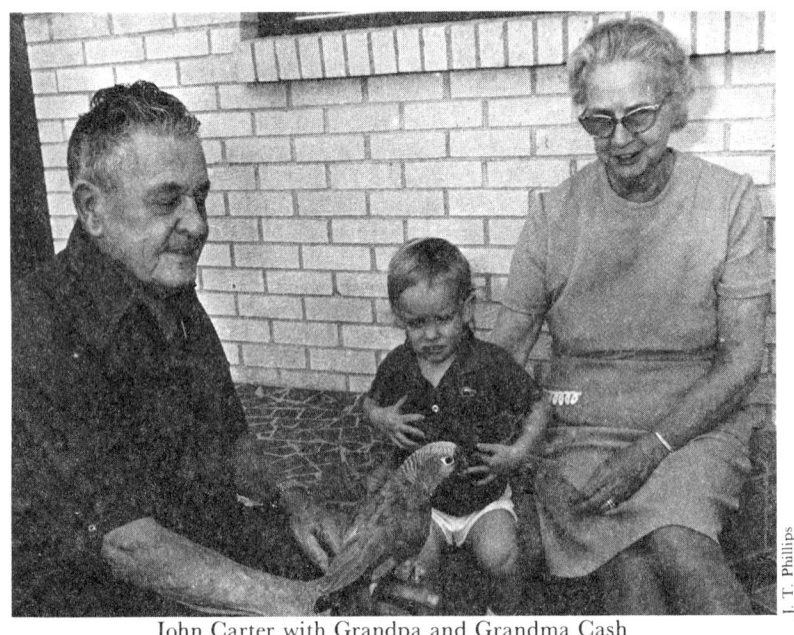

John Carter with Grandpa and Grandma Cash

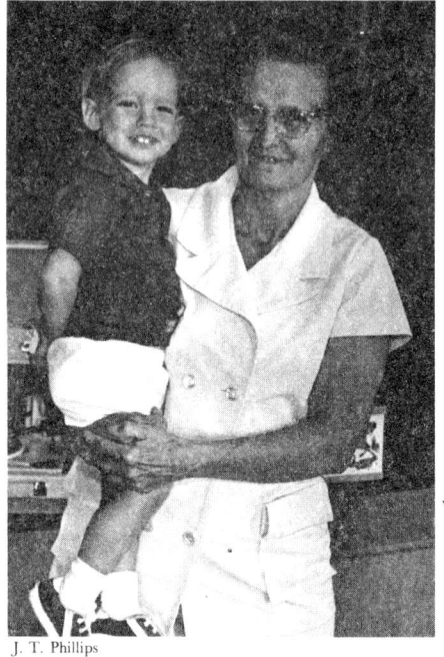

With Kelley

With George T.,
Kelley's husband

I've heard our friend Billy Graham say that his wife Ruth raised their children with a switch in one hand and a Bible in the other. I'm like Ruth and most mothers I think. I still believe a young child needs a little switch at times if what you are trying to get across to the child is very important. If my child runs across the street, taking dangerous chances, putting himself in danger of losing his life by accident, then a switch is a good reminder for his own good not to do that again. It could save his life. These are not beatings that I'm speaking of; sometimes the danger of child abuse comes too close to home for all of us.

What causes a parent to beat a child? Probably not the thing the child has just done. It could be the father has had a bad day at the office, and the end result is the back of the hand for some innocent little child.

Or the mother's bored with the washing, the ironing, the house cleaning—the things that so often drive a woman crazy wondering if her life has any meaning except drudgery. This can sometimes culminate at the end of a paddle on an innocent child's legs.

I think the place to start teaching our children is the Bible, God's rules for a good life. There are rights and wrongs, and they are all laid out through the Holy Spirit in the blessed Word of God. His way should be ours.

Then we should listen to our children. They are people, too. We should advise, with much prayer, if the problem is great. We should commit our children to God even before they are born—and claim the promise that our house will be saved.

We should read to them when they are small. John and I have used Bible stories with our children, and the Bible characters have become friends to our children along with lessons learned. Teach them the Word of God at a young age.

We've suffered a few failures in our lives with our six girls and one son, but we've always faced it head-on—John and I admitting that we've been as human as any of them. But we still are praying parents, and we thank God for some praying children, too.

We keep as many of our seven children with us as we can, although most of them are away from home. They are all in school or married or working on their own careers, so our travel is much different now. We have a large motor home so that we can have a home life together even on the road. This gives us that small palace of our own—a lot larger than that old back seat in our Packard, but the same ties are being bound to keep a family together.

We cook meals on the bus, stop at roadside parks, go to zoos, museums, and do all the things parents do with their children. In motels and hotels, we get a suite of rooms as close together as possible. Home can be the motor home, the back seat of a car, an airplane, or a suite in a motel. Home is where we are together.

I know my children will make their own mistakes. They'll scratch their own way through life. But I try to teach them the plan of salvation and claim that the Word of God is true, remembering that God, who cannot lie, promised life eternal before the world began. So this mother, remembering the old back-seat Packard days, tries to keep all her family together as much as possible, knowing that the children have heard the Holy Scriptures, praying that they will be made wise unto salvation through faith in Jesus Christ.

I function at home and while traveling only with the help of God. To be a believer, a Christian, is my first commitment. So I spend much time in prayer and study, asking God for the help it takes to run my family and my household. God has answered my prayers by sending me special people to help me in special ways. Kelley especially, my right arm with John Carter now that he is in school. And my household staff that enables me to work and spend the time with John that is necessary for our marriage and our work to be a success.

I must stay in a constant state of prayerfulness, because an active worker for Christ must have the guidance of the Holy Spirit. Sometimes the hardest thing for a mother to do is to keep her mouth shut when she should—oh, that God could bridle mine at times. I pray for compassion for others, for charity, love, and fellowship with my fellow-man.

In answer to a question once put to me—"How do you function?"—I try very hard to function for the Lord.

I know some folks would like to know more about our children—where they are, what they're doing, what's it been like to be a child of Johnny and June Cash—but those stories aren't mine to tell. What right do I have to infringe on the secrets of a twenty-one-year-old girl whose life is her own? That's her story to tell—or his, John Carter's. I cannot make my children's lives or testimonies mine; they belong to them.

Special Moments & People

My parents,
Mother Maybelle
and
Ezra J. Carter

My dad is seventy-three this year and not like anyone I
   know.
I've been in show business all my life, and only twice
   he's seen the show.
He's had so many things to do, he really hasn't had the
   time,
Starting way back years ago when he didn't have a
   dime.
He's always reading books, they come in every day,
He's an authority on the Bible, but he doesn't have much
   to say.*

I only saw the top of his head, his unruly hair sticking out, as we were rushing down the hall in the London airport. John, John Carter, Mother Maybelle, Kelley and George T., and Rosey and I—we were all running to get a plane for Germany. We had sailed on the *S. S. France* from New York and taken our good old wonderful time just sailing across the Atlantic, enjoying all that beautiful food. After gliding into Southampton a little late, we were rushing to make a date in Frankfurt, and there he was. My father.

Mother said, "I swear, I do believe that's Daddy with Helen and Anita," and sure enough, it was. It was one of the few times he chose to be a part of our concert tour. He wanted to visit the used book shops in London and look for old belt buckles. It was to be the last European tour Daddy ever made with us.

He had showed up just like that when we were going to Hawaii the last time. It was always a pleasure to have him because he was funny, and he was brilliant. He could talk about anything. He had studied law, elec-

This was written about my father a few years before he died.

tronics, mechanics, theology. He had even taken a job once as a cook on a shrimp boat. The whole Cash troupe loved having him when he chose to come along. Most of the boys and his close friends called him "Pop." He really was a free spirit.

Daddy saw John and me through some of the worst storms in life. He'd just cook another batch of biscuits, claim another promise in the Bible, and never let go.

>   There's things I've never done,
>   And more I'll never do,
>   Things I'll never see, or care to,
>   There's places I've never been,
>   People I'll never see,
>   But before I have to leave, Lord,
>   please let me
>   Spend one more summer in Virginia,
>   One more August in his arms,
>   Let me sit and rock on his front porch
>   and watch the nights go by.
>   Let me spend one more summer in Virginia
>   before I die.
>
>   Don Reid

Those Virginia mountains called to Daddy. An urgency that no one could explain drew him back there when we all thought he should take it a little easier, chop his garden with Mother, or go fishing at his place in Florida.

Why would he, at seventy-six years of age, want to return to that house where I was born and begin a more primitive life style again? But that's what he did. And we all pulled against that magnet to drag him back home to Tennessee because we knew he worked too hard there. He dug rocks, cleaned, nailed, and took on the rugged tasks of a pioneer again. He was tireless. But there was nothing we could say that would keep him safe and secure in Tennessee with us.

He would return to Virginia. It was as if he knew it was his last year. Then after chopping in 102-degree weather, he complained of shortness of breath, and Mother—over his protest—called us all and we took him to the hospital.

For five months he was in Madison Hospital—heart attacks, pacemakers, strokes, cardiac arrests, blood clots. He should have died twenty times, but he wouldn't. I think we prayed him alive. We couldn't let him go. We believed he would live, so we *wouldn't* let him go. That poor old man who was so indestructible could not die.

They suggested we put him in a nursing home, and we just couldn't do that. Oh, I'm sure there are fine places for the sick to go and stay and that the care is good, but we took him home. A man should, if possible, be allowed to die with dignity in his own home. And so we took on the almost impossible task of finding registered nurses, twenty-four hours a day. They said it couldn't be done, but it was, with the help of Uncle Toob, Aunt Babe, Peggy Knight, and Mother. We had, our own hospital. After five weeks at home, Daddy returned to the hospital again. It was heartbreaking to see him reduced to speechlessness—the loss of weight—and the look of despair and wanting to die in his eyes.

Then I got a terrible case of strep throat, and I just gave up. God finally let me say, "Praise God, and take Daddy home"—and He did. Daddy was gone.

Daddy's bedroom was always an unusual sight. He put it on and wore it! Daddy loved to lie in his bed and read. He had bookshelves all around his head, all around each wall, and across the ceiling. While wearing his bedroom, he could reach his favorite book from the flat of his back. He sometimes slept in the bed with twenty-five or thirty books—and Mother Maybelle.

Daddy didn't leave me gold or silver
Or rich lands and keys,
But he did leave me a yearning
For the Word and falling on my knees.

And books and books of Jesus,
Moses, Abraham and God,
A love for things eternal
Not built here on this sod.

For Daddy didn't care about earthly
 things,
He studied a better place,
His books were piled in closets,
In cases around his bed,
And falling in your face.

Momma tried to pick them up
And find them a home upon a shelf.
Since Daddy's gone to the better place,
I find I'm reading them all myself.

I study about the Apostle Paul—
Daddy had a thousand books about
 that man,
And what the commentators didn't know
Is written there in Daddy's hand.

So rest in peace, dear Daddy,
When Jesus comes to save,
We'll all be rising up to heaven
When you come busting from your grave.

As the angels herald their coming
At the brightness of the Son,
I'll be richer then in wisdom
As we're rising up as one.

Mountain lady, do you sit on your front porch in the cool of the day?
Mountain lady, did you think your kids would ever come back to stay?
Mountain lady, does the columbine still twine around your door,
And did you ever get a rug to cover the cracks where my diaper drug on your wooden floor?
Mountain lady, does the country churchbell ring on Sunday morn?
Mountain lady, do you still wear that old apron, ragged and torn?
Mountain lady, on winter nights before our old fireplace,
As you look into the flames, do you ever call my name and do you see my face?

    Oh, you Appalachian lady,
    Once I was your little baby,
    And you rocked me in your homemade rocking chair.
    Since I heard the wild goose calling,
    I have done a lot of falling.
    Mountain lady, someday I'll come to you there.

By Johnny Cash—for my mother

My mother's favorite song was "Wildwood Flower." I can still hear that melody as she played and sang it.

I don't remember Mother ever complaining about anything. In the beginning when we traveled together, she drove the car, made all our clothes and washed and ironed them, along with all the singing and recording.

Mother never knew she was special. She just was. I don't remember anyone not loving my mother. Those pale blue mountain eyes gathered all those near around her, and her humble, simple life style never changed.

She loved laughing with us, almost like a young girl herself. The four of us—Helen, Anita, Mother, and I—grew together, and that haunting sound of songs like "Little Joe the Wrangler," "Give Me the Roses While I Live," or "Forsaken Lover" took on a great importance for us, with the simple lyrics and Mother's guitar. There was a purity about her music that made Mother stand as the master of a new school which we were to call "hillbilly" music. Later she became the mother figure to the folk generation. The love she gave spread throughout our business, and many of our country music people referred to her only as "Mother." And down through the years she earned that title.

An era is gone now. Mother is gone. She died October 23, 1978, leaving the world mourning the death of a legend—a simple little 5'2" Appalachian lady whose haunting blue eyes will shine in our memories, whose pure music still endures.

I've always believed that God takes the very good, the godly, in their sleep. And that's the way she went—quietly, not a move or a struggle—in her sleep. She was still so beautiful, looking forty-five instead of her sixty-nine years. But she was tired from the time Daddy died; it was as if some of Mother died when he left us.

Helen, Anita, and I moved over to share our grief with Peggy Knight, who had nursed Mother for over four years. Then we took another step to make room for Jan Howard, who sings as part of our Carter Family. It was as if there was not room enough or steps enough to take to cover the space it took for her grieving loved ones—John, Bob, Glenn—her grandchildren and great-grandchildren, her friends, and people she never knew. We mourn her death, yet we have the satisfaction of knowing she has life eternal.

God has picked His wildwood flower.

Mother and her autoharp

1974—
Mother received
the Tex Ritter Award

Left to right: Me, Anita, Dad, Mother, Helen

Left to right: Danny Jones (Helen's son), Rosey, Helen, John, Me, Rosanne Cash, David Jones (Helen's son), and Mother Maybelle

Helen, Mother, and I

Have you ever felt that you just had to do something? That's the way I felt about our movie *Gospel Road*. I'd had a dream about seeing my John standing on a mountain somewhere in the Holy Land—and the picture would not leave my mind. He stood there on that mountain, his hair streaming in the breeze, and he talked about Jesus. There was no way I could rest until the dream became a reality. We knew nothing about making a movie. But if it took all our life, if it took every cent we had, if it took us away from this earth, we had to go to Israel and do that film.

We wanted to do a movie about the life of Christ, told in a simple way so that somehow the world would know what we believed. It was to be made like a documentary, with John telling about Jesus and singing most of the songs.

There were miracles of all kinds around us as we filmed. The biggest miracle was that we were able to do the film at all, with the unrest in Arab-Israeli relations. We worked eighteen hours a day, and daily God showed us what to do. We had a pretty good script—the Bible. The Arabs and Israelis worked together to help us, and a Hand stronger than ours directed our movie.

I really saw it—a florescent-like figure that moved behind John, walking around him and over toward the sun and back again. I saw it that early morning as John stood on top of the mountain and the cameras rolled to film the opening scene of *Gospel Road*. It was a hazy time with the sun shining through the sand and mist blowing over the Qumran, and I hesitated to mention what I saw. "They'll never believe me," I said to myself. "No one will believe me." But there it was.

I'd never seen anything like it in my life. I closed my eyes. I looked again, and there it stood; this figure—

maybe twenty-five-feet high—moving to and fro. I felt as if I were in a dream. I had seen John on that mountain in my dream—and there he was now—and it all looked the same except for that figure. How could I explain it? No one else seemed to see it.

I thought about Larry Butler. He had his head on straight. He was doing the music with John for the film, and there he stood with all his senses under control. I called to him.

"Larry, come here." He walked away from Brother Snow, Larry Lee (playing John the Baptist), and Reba and came over to me.

I asked him quietly, "Larry, I know this sounds crazy, but I really think I can see something—a florescent figure walking behind John. They'll all think I'm crazy, but do you see anything?"

Butler took a good look, then said, "Don't be silly, June. I can't see anything."

I said, "Just keep looking."

He must have stood by me fifteen minutes, then suddenly dropping to his knees, he yelled, "Oh, my God, I can see it, too!"

All I know is that I saw it, Larry Butler saw it, Reba saw it, Brother Snow saw it, and Larry Lee saw it. I don't know what it was, but it was there. We took it as a sign that God was giving us His blessing on the movie *Gospel Road*.

It took months to edit the film, and our friends encouraged us—Billy Graham, Larry Gatlin, Marshall Grant, Kris Kristofferson. Then came the important business of choosing songs. Some were done by the Statler Brothers, some with the Carter Family singing background, but most of the songs were sung by John. When the film was released, it began touching lives everywhere. God still had His hand on it.

There was a time years ago when I didn't seem to be scared of anything. I'd fly all over in small airplanes with Helen's boyfriend, now her husband, Glenn Jones. We did tailspins, nose dives, back and forward loops, and I laughed my head off. We took the top off our old willow tree at Glen Allen, Virginia, and I always thought it was funny. Later I flew to and from New York every week, and all over the United States.

And then, on March 5, 1963, I lost four very special people all at the same time—Hawkshaw Hawkins, Cowboy Copas, Randy Hughes, and Patsy Cline.

Patsy had stayed with me some time before she started working at the Grand Ole Opry. She had talent, and was no hypocrite about anything. She'd call sometimes for moral support and say, "Talk to me, June, just about Jesus. Just talk." We did tours together, and she had just started to become a big star. We had laughed and cried many times together. She was a friend I really cared about. Once we were on tour in California and she said to me, "I don't have long to live." I didn't believe her.

For years Hawkshaw Hawkins had teased me, and he'd been in my home to eat at my table many times. I'd known him even before the Opry at Wheeling, West Virginia, and he always cared about my ups and downs—because he was having his, too. He was always just Hawk, who'd stop and talk on Saturdays about his tours or his life, his spiritual highs and lows. We shared a lot.

One summer, Cowboy Copas and I had done a fair season together. All summer we played Kansas, Nebraska, and Missouri fairs. He missed his wife, Lucille, and his family, and I missed my daughter Carlene. We rode many a mile together and became real buddies.

Randy Hughes was just one of the young men who hung around Anita and I after the early morning shows on WSM. He'd come eat breakfast at our house, and he'd go on show dates with us in the Tennessee area. He wanted to play bass and guitar, and he did very well. He was dear to our family and went with us on many trips. He had recently married Cathy Copas, Cowboy's daughter.

And then it happened. One night in a storm, on the way home from Kansas City where these four had been together to do a benefit for a disc jockey's family, the plane carrying these four dear friends went down in western Tennessee, and they were all dead and gone—all at one time. It was one of the saddest days the Grand Ole Opry had ever known. I grieved for one and then the other. They were all gone—all these special people of mine at the same time—and I've never quite gotten over it.

Since then I have not been able to fly with any peace of mind. Even after all our trips across the United States and around the world, I am frightened to death of an airplane. Oh, I fly. I rebuke Satan for the fear, and I pray, but I sweat and I shake all over, and many times when the weather is bad I just pass out from fear saying Psalm 91. This must surely be the "thorn in my flesh," to quote Paul, and only God can deliver me from it. It's something I live with, and I fight it with God's help.

I think this is the way Satan works. He finds our weak spots and runs to and fro trying to claim us in a moment of weakness. So I quote all the Scripture, I remember all the promises, and I know there are prayer groups that cover us with prayer all the time.

I firmly believe that the angels walk with me. That's a pretty big statement for me to make, but there's no way this old Appalachian girl with a puritan soul can survive two broken marriages and go through the ups and downs of life without knowing Someone stronger and greater than man has His hand on my life. In my most troubled times, the angels picked me up seven times—and when I'd think there was no way for peace of mind, I finally gave it all to God. I just let go. He handled it for me.

I sometimes call myself a Seventh Day Adventist Baptist Methodist Pentecostal Jew. I believe the seventh day is Sabbath. I was raised a Methodist. I still believe in once-saved-always-saved from my years in the Baptist church. I believe in the indwelling of the Holy Spirit, and I find myself an ingrafted Jew because of the promise to the Gentiles.

I really don't know too much about doctrines. I try to live my life each day holding my hand up to God for His support and looking for a way to grow in the Word and the Spirit. I just simply believe in God and Jesus. The Holy Spirit is my comforter—and I trust God to reveal to me the things that are good and truth.

I've always feared that the singing, the dancing, the show business of my life would somehow wage a great war between Satan and myself. I used to think it was his playground, his hometown, his home base, that it belonged to him. Now I've gone that forty years in the wilderness with him. I've wandered, made mistakes, and God has always brought me back again to the simple faith of a child. I know now that this great stage of life is one where the scene is played over and over, and I'm no longer lukewarm or on the fence. I'm on God's side. There I stand and wait until He calls me.

I don't stand on the stage and shout the glories of heaven or preach to my friends. I've shared more of how I feel about Christ in this book than I've ever done before. My object has always been to just live as good a life as I could and to answer questions about my faith and to witness only if the power of the Holy Spirit gave me the words to do so. Most of the time I've been silent around my friends for fear I would be too overzealous and scare them off. My prayer is still that my friends will feel and know that I know and love God and that Christ is the only way for our eternal life.

I am happy—you know, it sounds strange to write it down—but it took a lot of mistakes, a lot of hurt, a lot of learning and praying on my part, and I'm still trying to find my full purpose in this life. Daily it's a new commitment. The hardest thing for me still is to keep my mouth shut at times. I still love to entertain, to perform, to act. It's a challenge to pick the right material, to always do the right thing, so my mistakes mount just as yours do. But He is always there to help and guide. It's rough just being a Christian in this world today, but I keep remembering that Christ died for people like me—me with all my "mounted up" mistakes.

It's a wonderful feeling to be in front of a receptive audience. I never go on the stage without first stopping in the wings and giving thanks for the opportunity of just being there. I pray that in some way someone in the audience will know and feel that there is something special in the lives of June and Johnny Cash that makes them want to entertain, to share a part of themselves with the audience. I pray that a special spirit will be evident when we sing the gospel songs, that there will be true meaning in our love songs, and that the audience will sense that Johnny Cash can identify with almost all the people who come to our concerts.

Our lives are entwined with the people over the footlights; we are a part of them. And even though we try to change some material or add a new dimension to our show, the old songs are the ones most requested. "I Walk the Line," "Ring of Fire," "Jackson," "If I Were a Carpenter"—all of these are requested again and again. So we sing them with as much gusto as we did the first time.

I reach now for a spiritual feeling near the end of the show, because I do give my performance—good or bad—to God. I thank Him and praise Him in my spirit and pray that someone will know Christ lives within me. I really don't preach this, even to my best friends. I just pray they will see the difference in my life and in John's and stop to ask the question: What is this special thing that makes you happy? What is this special glow you have? The answer is peace. The peace of God through the love of the Lord Jesus Christ.

Sometimes my bones still hurt from the touring of one-night stands.
>	Green Bay, Wisconsin
>	Rockford, Illinois
>	Madison, Wisconsin
>	Topeka, Kansas
>	University of Missouri
>	Kansas City, Kansas
>	Wichita, Kansas
>	Salina, Kansas
>	Amarillo, Texas
>	Phoenix, Arizona
>	Pueblo, Colorado
>	El Paso, Texas

How many more? I can't remember. There must be a place for rest somewhere. John, Kelley, Brother Tom, John Carter, Mike Woosley, Marshall Grant, and I—a trip in the motor home across the Navajo reservation. The Monument Valley, the Valley of the Gods, the Colorado Rockies, snow storms—more aches and pains from my back. Drive to Omaha. Take a plane to Chicago. Home—record—write—be a mother—pray—breathe. And finally it's today—it's all right. Up at 4:00 A.M. Work on book. Cook breakfast for John Carter—almost six now. He's gone to school.

I'm amazed at John's energy. He's talking about doing a new television show. More recording for him today. We're working on the life of Paul.

My home is so full of antiques now. A collector like me just keeps on making more room and overcrowding things. John's taken some wonderful photos for my book—his new hobby makes him happy.

Got to pick up Aunt Polly's dancing shoes. I should never have let John see that crazy character. He's had me doing her on all the last concerts. She even recorded with him yesterday. She's spirited, but she makes me tired.

Oh, well, it's eight o'clock and there's a day ahead of me. Must talk to Virgil about the rose garden. Help me, God, to live each day for You.

<hr>

"For ever, O Lord, thy word is settled in heaven" (Psalm 119:89).

<hr>

"For the promise is unto you, and to your children, and to all that are afar off, even as many as the Lord our God shall call" (Acts 2:39).

I don't have much time now to lie on my back and search the clouds. My horizon has gone beyond the mountains to include the world, from Green Bay, Wisconsin, to Frankfurt, Germany. I have done wonderful things through the power of God. And I have done foolish things in my own power. And He has loved me and forgiven me.

I have met kings and queens and presidents. I have tried to share my wonderful Christ with the world.

I don't have much time now to lie on my back and search the clouds, and life to me is much more than four square miles. But the face of Jesus is still very special to me, and I am still His special speck of sand. And my loved ones are very special to Him. All my klediments.

I wrote so many chapters for this book—like "Jan and Job" for my friend Jan Howard; "Joy and Jessi" for Jessi Colter, the wife of friend Waylon Jennings; "Eternal Ease and Esther" for my cousin Esther Moore; chapters and chapters for Fluke Holland, our drummer, "Come On, Penni, Come On" for my hairdresser Penni Lane; "Luck and Luther" for Luther Perkins, John's guitar player who died several years ago; "Faith in Frances" for friend Frances Lyell—so many people who helped my life be what it is today. But these stories are complete books in their own way, so I just thank these friends for being a part of my life.

Most of all I'd like to thank Irene Gibbs, John's secretary, for all the hours of typing, Reba Hancock, who helped me gather all these photos, and my new-found friend, Judy Markham, who edited this book and let me keep all this in my own words and say it in my own way. I prayed God would give me that special person—He did—and thanks again to Judy.

Ray and Carrie Cash, John's parents

Our dear friends, Roland and Marie Wolf, in 1972 at Opryland

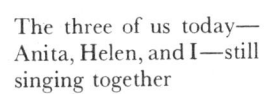

The three of us today—Anita, Helen, and I—still singing together

Our farm in Bon Aqua

Our home in Jamaica—Cinnamon Hill

As Mary Magdalene in
"Gospel Road"

On the set of
"Little House on the Prairie"

Filming the "Great American Train
Story" in Utah

Another birthday

Tadeusz Dabrowski

our grandchildren

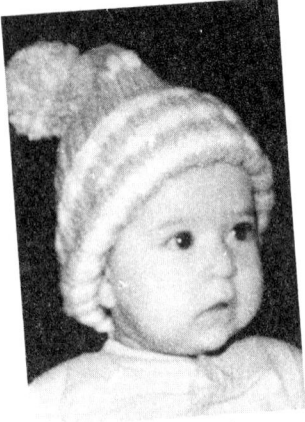

Jessica Brock
Cindy's daughter

Thomas Gabriel Coggins
Kathy's son

Tiffany Simpkins
Carlene's daughter

John Jackson Routh
Carlene's son